*1.25

123637

C. LESLIE
MILLER All

About
Angels

16163

G/L
REGAL
BOOKS

A Division of G/L Publications
Glendale, California, U.S.A.

The Scripture quotations, other than the *King James Version*, are from the *New American Standard Bible*. © by The Lockman Foundation, La Habra, Calif., 1960, 1971. Used by permission.

© Copyright 1973 by G/L Publications
All rights reserved.
Printed in the U.S.A.

Published by
Regal Books Division, G/L Publications
Glendale, California 91209, U.S.A.

Library of Congress Catalog No. 73-82096
ISBN 0-8307-0257-1

Contents

Acknowledgments

It is impossible to thank by name the many persons who submitted to interviews or provided written accounts of visions, dreams, or appearances of creatures of light which seemed to be related to angelic manifestations. The sources of the materials used are acknowledged in the footnotes or the text. I owe personal thanks to Mr. William T. Greig, Jr., for the encouragement and title he provided; to Dr. Wilbur M. Smith for his assistance with the bibliography and the use of his extensive library; to Miss Eleanor Doan, Mr. Dan Peters, Mrs. Charla Pereau, Mrs. Kay Gudnason, Mrs. Hope Friedmann, Mrs. John Hunter and Mr. Gary Greig for bringing useful material to my attention; and to Mrs. Myrtle Perry for uncomplainingly typing and retyping the manuscript.

Introduction

Why write a book about angels? The simple answer is, because no books are being written about them.

Books by the score are being written about the Satan cult, witchcraft, spiritism, astrology and every other kindred subject. Courses on witchcraft are being offered in universities. The secular, as well as the Christian, world is being made aware of the presence and activities of invisible, sinister creatures, citizens of a kingdom of darkness. Scientists are beginning to admit the possibility of the existence of some form of invisible intelligence and are taking measures to probe into phenomena and manifestations which cannot be explained by any law known to present-day science.

It cannot be denied that a mysterious and practically unexplored dimension exists, which in the Bible is defined as "principalities and powers of darkness."

This dimension is exciting dangerous curiosity on the part of many people and apprehension on the part of those who have some knowledge of the Word of God.

But is it not strange that all this curiosity and investigation is concentrated on the evil and negative continent of the spirit world? If such a negative form exists, is it not reasonable to believe there is also a positive and benevolent form of spirit life? And if there is, what are these creatures like? Are they here on earth? What do they look like? Have they exerted a significant influence in human history? Do they still become involved in human life and destiny?

The *hundreds* of times such "good spirits" from the other side of the spirit world are mentioned in the Bible would seem to indicate that both the Author and the scribes of the Bible believed in their existence and importance. In fact, references to angels far outnumber references to demons, evil spirits and Satan. And if they are so important, why don't we hear more about them and about what they do, or, are willing to do for God's children today?

These are the questions which prompted this writer to attempt to discover some answers. By no means does he claim to provide most of the answers. Only the Spirit of God, He who came to lead and guide us into *all* truth, can do that. Even He may defer some answers until we "know as we are known."

In accumulating the record of human experiences in relation to angels, great care has been taken to use only such material as could be documented or which came from sources where integrity and reliability cannot be questioned. Extensive correspondence and interviews brought to light many interesting experiences, but most of these consisted of visions and dreams without supporting witnesses. Several personal encounters with God's Holy Ones have been included and for these the writer begs the reader's indulgence.

In the following pages almost every reference in God's Word dealing with angels is brought to the attention of the reader, and hopefully that he will be led thereby to realize the great importance and the extent of heaven's angels in biblical history, in contemporary Christian experiences and in the ages to come. And even more important, that this investigation will lead the reader beyond the dimension of angels into the presence of the One who created them for His own pleasure and to serve as ministering servants to those redeemed by the blood of the Lamb.

CHAPTER 1

There Are Two Sides

It was an unusual prayer, both in content and in location. "Lord, cause now Thine angels to surround me; and let them not be transparent today, for the guards must not see me."

When Corrie ten Boom and her sister Betsie arrived as Dutch prisoners at the dreaded Ravensbruck prison camp, all possessions, including clothing, were to be taken from them by the Nazi guards.

Relating the horrible indignities and privations they suffered, she writes: "Together we entered the terrifying building. At a table were women who took away all our possessions. Everyone had to undress completely and then go to a room where her hair was clipped short.

"I asked a guard who was busy checking the possessions of the new arrivals if I might use the toilet. She pointed to a door to the showers. . . . Betsie stayed close beside me all the time. Suddenly I had an inspiration. 'Quick, take off your woolen underwear,' I whispered to her. I rolled it up with mine and laid the bundle in a corner with my little Bible. The spot was alive with cockroaches, but I didn't worry about that. I felt wonderfully relieved and happy. 'The Lord is busy answering our prayers, Betsie,' I whispered, 'we shall not have to make the sacrifice of all our clothes.'

"We hurried back to the row of women waiting to be undressed. A little later, after we had our showers and put on our shirts and shabby dresses, I hid the roll of underwear and my Bible under my dress. It did bulge out obviously through my dress; but I prayed, 'Lord, cause now Thine angels to surround me; and let them not be transparent today, for the guards must not see me.' I felt perfectly at ease. Calmly I passed the guards. Everyone was checked, from the front, the sides, the back. Not a bulge escaped the eyes of the guard. The woman just in front of me had hidden a woolen vest under her dress; it was taken from her. They let me pass, for they did not see me. Betsie, right behind me, was searched.

"But outside awaited another danger. On each side of the door were women who looked everyone over for a second time. They felt over the body of each one who passed. I knew they would not see me, for the angels were still surrounding me. I was not even surprised when they passed me by; but within me rose the jubilant cry, 'O Lord, if Thou dost so answer prayer, I can face even Ravensbruck unafraid.' "[1]

One of the most alarming phenomena of our culture is the growing interest in the occult and witchcraft. Satan is not only alive, he is being worshiped

2

openly and on an ever-widening scale. The drug culture is drifting into the demon culture. Thousands of young people are being drawn into this deadly maelstrom where all personal liberty and control is lost, and the body, mind and soul of the victim becomes the habitation and tool of vile spirit beings.

But there is another side to the world of spirits. Not all spirits are evil, nor are the good spirits inactive. They surrounded Corrie ten Boom with a shield of invisibility in the Nazi prison camp. They have been active in every period of human history and they are active here and now.

It may be unfortunate that so many books, pamphlets and magazine articles on demons and Satan worship are being published today while the other side of the world of spirits is almost completely ignored. Also, little or nothing is being written about the "disguised" aspect of satanic activity to which the apostle Paul referred when he wrote, "Even Satan disguises himself as an angel of light. Therefore it is not surprising if his servants also disguise themselves as servants of righteousness; whose end shall be according to their deeds."[2]

Little attention is being drawn to these dangerous disguises, yet they may be more dangerous than the overt activities of the kingdom of darkness:

The substitution of a social gospel for the message of repentance toward God and faith in the Lord Jesus Christ; the emphasis upon form, program and method in worship; the permissive dissertations of teachers having ears which "itch" for compliments and acceptance;[3] the priority of materialism and tolerance. These are some of the disguises used by the "angel of light" in his efforts to deceive the very elect.[4] Little is being said and less is being printed exposing this "white" form of satanic activity.

It is true that in order to oppose the enemy we must be able to recognize him. But we should be careful lest we make the mistake that C. S. Lewis describes in *The Screwtape Letters.* "There are two equal and opposite errors into which our race can fall about the devils. One is to disbelieve in their existence, the other is to believe and to feel an unhealthy interest in them! They themselves are equally pleased by both errors, and they hail a materialist or a magician with the same delight."[5]

It is reasonable to believe that as we approach the end of the "end times," there will be increasing activity on the part of demons and bolder aggressiveness by the "prince of the power of the air." It is equally reasonable to believe that there will be corresponding activity on the part of God's Holy Ones. This activity may not be visual, but will probably manifest itself in supernatural displays and inexplicable circumstances in the areas of deliverance, political events and providential provision. God has never gone out of the miracle business. As the Second Appearing of Christ approaches, we may expect to see more and more demonstrations of His miraculous power. In these demonstrations it is likely that He will use angels as He has done so frequently in the past.

Horace M. Du Bose, in *The Bible and the Ages,* writes, "For one, I am inclined to expect in the very last days of the world's regeneration, a renewal of angelic visitations to those who shall be heirs of salvation."

4

It is important that Christians discover the reality and the functions of the other side of the spirit world. They need to recognize how frequently and to what a great extent the Holy Ones have influenced the destiny of men and nations in the past. The Bible brings angels to our attention about three hundred times. In so doing, it provides an amazing amount of information about them. It is also important that Christians discover that angels are appearing, are protecting, are supplying the needs and ministering in multitudes of ways to God's children *today!*

Undoubtedly, their presence in times of danger and their interference when the powers of darkness launch an attack have made the difference in thousands of instances between fatality or deliverance, defeat or victory.

Footnotes to Chapter 1

1. Corrie ten Boom, *A Prisoner and Yet* (Fort Washington, Pa.: Christian Literature Crusade, London, 1954).
2. 2 Corinthians 11:14,15
3. 2 Timothy 4:3
4. Matthew 24:24
5. C. S. Lewis, *The Screwtape Letters* (New York: The Macmillan Co., 1969), p. 3.

CHAPTER 2

Angels as Persons

Are angels real? Do they have form? Are they visible? What are their activities? What is their relation to men and to this world? Do intelligent people really believe that they exist?

Oswald Chambers, in *His Life and Work,* wrote, "As I walked through the lines tonight, alone in this mighty desert, under the serene dome of sky and the wonderful stars, I realized again the unique sense of the presence of angels. I noticed it repeatedly the first time I went abroad. It is quite distinct from the certainty that God is guarding, this is the beautiful sense of angel presence. Anyway, that is how it strikes me and I thank God for it."

Some men may question the reality of angel creatures, while many believe, and a few even experience personal contact with those beings of mystery, called by Daniel, "the Holy Ones."

The only reliable source of information concerning

the existence, the history, the activities, the power and the present ministries of angels is God's Holy Word. Many of the answers to our questions are there. We know not, because we search not in the Scriptures concerning these Holy Ones.

Much of what we know about angels comes to us from the book of Hebrews. There they are presented in contrast to the person and position of the Lord Jesus Christ, and in saying what they are NOT, there is much revealed to us as to what they are.

Angels Are Created, Not Begotten

Referring to Christ, the writer of Hebrews asks, "To which of the angels did He ever say,

'Thou art My Son,

Today I have begotten Thee'?

And again,

'I will be a Father to Him,

And He shall be a Son to Me'?

And when He again brings the first-born into the world, He says,

'And let all the angels of God worship Him.'

And of the angels He says,

'Who makes His angels winds,

And His ministers a flame of fire.'

But of the Son He says,

'Thy throne, O God, is forever and ever,

And the righteous scepter is the scepter of

His kingdom.

'Thou hast loved righteousness and hated lawlessness;

Therefore God, Thy God, hath anointed Thee

With the oil of gladness above Thy companions.'

8

And

'Thou, Lord, in the beginning didst lay the
foundation of the earth,
And the heavens are the works of Thy hands;
They will perish, but Thou remainest;
And they all will become old as a garment,
And as a mantle Thou wilt roll them up;
As a garment they will also be changed.
But Thou art the same,
And Thy years will not come to an end.'
But to which of the angels has He ever said,
'Sit at My right hand,
Until I make Thine enemies
A footstool for Thy feet'?
Are they not all ministering spirits, sent out to
render service for the sake of those who will inherit
salvation?"[1]

There is much mystery shrouding the identity of
angels—the Holy Ones—created as a special order of
spirit beings. Their origin is found in the Living Word
of whom it is said, "For in Him all things were
created, both in the heavens and on earth, visible
and invisible . . . all things have been created through
Him and for Him."[2]

The existence of spirit entities has been basic in
almost all systems of religion and superstitious mis-
conceptions of such beings have served as the womb
for the development of most forms of idolatry.

In *Christian Theology* (5th edition), Dr. William
Cooke comments:

"Indeed, in nearly all the systems of religion, ancient or modern, we trace such beings. . . . We have
abundant evidence of almost universal belief in the

existence of spiritual intelligences, ranging in different orders between man and his Maker. Here, however, we often find truth draped in fiction, and facts distorted by the wildest fancies of mythology.

"Heathen philosophers and poets often spoke of the ministry of spiritual beings. Socrates often spoke of a good demon attending him, and directing and guiding him by his admonitions. Plato taught that the higher kind of demons, such as had never dwelt in mortal bodies, were appointed guardians unto men. But old Hesiod ascribes a ministering agency to the spirits that had once inhabited mortal bodies during the golden age, and speaks of them as:

Aerial spirits, by great Jove design'd
To be on earth the guardians of mankind,
Invisible to mortal eyes they go,
And mark our actions good or bad below;
The immortal spies with watchful care preside,
And twice ten thousand round their charges glide;
They can reward with glory or with gold,
A power they by divine permission hold.

"We have here a brief representation of that general sentiment on the offices of these superior beings, which we find so abundantly amplified in the speculations of philosophers, and the dreamy fictions of the poets. But with what steadfast foot we tread when, leaving the flitting theories and amusing dramas of the heathen, we come to the substantial verities of revelation, and in the narrative of simple truth hear what God has said and saints have seen of the angel world."

Jesus informed us that angels do not procreate and have no marriage relations,[3] neither can they experience death.[4] Paul tells us in 1 Corinthians 13 that they have their own language, and Jude writes that they have their own divinely appointed abode and domain.

While the Holy Ones are pure spirit,[5] they do have form. A body must not necessarily be of flesh and bone. In his great treatise on the Resurrection in 1 Corinthians 15, the apostle Paul wrote about "heavenly bodies" and he also emphasized, "There is also a spiritual body."

Angels are able to partake of food. In reciting the miracle of the manna eaten by Israel during their wilderness wanderings, the Psalmist refers to the manna as "the bread of angels."[6] There is the possibility that this was more than poetic fancy. When the Lord and His two Holy Ones appeared to Abraham by the oaks of Mamre, they accepted his hospitality and ate of the roast veal and bread prepared by Sarah.[7]

With a touch of humor and with a great deal of truth Halford E. Luccock wrote in *The Christian Century:* "We so often hear the expression 'the voice of an angel' that I got to wondering what an angel would sound like. So I did some research, and discovered that an angel's voice sounds remarkably like a person saying, 'Hurry up!'

"Until the time I took over, research had been blocked because it was based on the delusion that the voice of an angel would always be beautiful. The words 'Get up' are rarely beautiful, never less so than at 7 A.M. Yet that is what the angels always say when they talk to men, as reported in the Bible. I can't think of anything an angel ever said but 'Get up and hurry!' An angel comes to Peter in jail and says, 'Rise quickly.' An angel says to Gideon, 'Arise and go in this thy might.' An angel appears to Joseph in a dream, when Herod is slaughtering the infants, and says, 'Go quickly.' An angel appears to Philip and says, 'Arise and go.'

"Really, the angels are monotonous talkers! They always say the same thing—'Arise, hurry!' But so is a fire bell monotonous. If we are to be saved, it will be by monotony, the reiterated command, 'Get up and get going!'

"Listen carefully and you can hear the voice of angels above the contemporary din of the world, a voice that ought to get us out of lounge chairs and comfortable beds. 'Arise, go quickly!'

"It might be a good idea to allow an angel to occupy the pulpit on Sunday. An irate hearer said to Samuel Barnett when he was canon of Bristol Cathedral in England, 'I come to church to be comforted, and you sound like a fire alarm.' Perhaps there was a fire."

Although usually invisible to men, angels have appeared in human form upon many occasions.[x] In later chapters we will examine some of these appearances. When visible to men they resembled young men; and they never were described as beautiful young women or as having wings.

Someone has suggested that angels are visible, but our eyes are not made to see them. Human sight is adjusted to only a small portion of the light waves and is far from being perfect or complete. Animals and birds see and hear things beyond our range of sight and hearing.

But there have been many times in the past when

God permitted human eyes to focus in on heaven's light rays and actually see the heavenly bodies of angels. At other times the Holy Ones assumed human form and were seen in the physical appearance and dress of the culture of the person who was the object of the divine visitation. Nor was this confined to the past. The same thing happens today!

A Christian electrician related the following incident. "In 1965 the Lakeview Terrace Baptist Church in California bought a two-story residence which they proceeded to renovate so that it could be used for worship. I was engaged to do the electrical work. One morning I was working on a ladder at the top of the steps to the second floor. Although I had not heard anyone coming up the old creaky steps, I was suddenly aware of another presence—that someone was watching me. I glanced down and there was a man standing at the foot of the ladder. He was clean but poorly dressed and asked if he could secure employment from me. I told him he would have to see the contractor who, at the time, was not available. For just a fraction of a second I turned my head when suddenly the thought came to me, 'This man may be hungry or in need.' Immediately I looked down to offer my assistance but he was not there! He could not have gone down the steps without my seeing or hearing him. I got off the ladder, ran down the steps and outside the building but he was nowhere in sight. Returning to the house I looked in every room, and then again looked outside. This building was surrounded by empty lots and there was no place for even a dog to hide. The stranger had disappeared!"

Was the stranger one of the Holy Ones? I do not know, but I do know Tom, the electrician. And I know that never since has he hesitated for one moment in generously helping anyone in need.

Angels May Be Seen by Beasts

Many hundreds of years ago, a gentile prophet chose the permissive will of God and was on his way to curse the Israelites. Suddenly his faithful beast of burden balked; then, a little further down the road, he balked again and crushed the prophet's foot against a stone wall. When the prophet cruelly beat the beast, the Lord gave it the power of speech and at the same time opened the eyes of the prophet to see what the mule had seen right along—an angel blocking the path, with a drawn sword in his hand. The mule was able to see the Holy One who had been invisible to Balaam.[9]

Angels Have Superhuman Powers

These Holy Ones possess superhuman powers. They are immune to flame and heat. Manoah, the father of the superman, Samson, saw an angel ascend in the flame of the altar.[10] Nebuchadnezzar, the king of Babylon, saw a Holy One walking unharmed with the three Hebrew children in his burning, fiery furnace.[11]

The apostle Peter wrote of angels as being "greater in might and power."[12] The Psalmist describes them as "Mighty in strength, who perform His word, obeying the voice of His word."[13]

Angels Are Free Moral Agents

Even though Jesus referred to these ministering

spirits as "holy angels,"[14] they are free moral agents and some of them have joined Lucifer in his rebellion against God.[15] Of these rebel spirits, Peter wrote, "God did not spare angels when they sinned, but cast them into hell and committed them to pits of darkness, reserved for judgment."[16] The apostle Jude, writing of the same sinful angels, informs us that, "angels who did not keep their own domain, but abandoned their proper abode, He has kept in eternal bonds under darkness for the judgment of the great day."[17]

Angels Are Limited in Knowledge

Even though these Holy Ones are greatly superior to man in power and glory, they have their limitations. Both Peter and Jesus call our attention to the fact that angels are limited in knowledge. They are not omniscient. Prior to the redemptive mission of the Lord Jesus Christ, and the birth of the church, angels sought in vain to unravel this mystery.[18] Jesus said that the angels are ignorant of the day and hour of His return in glory.[19]

In His story of Dives and Lazarus, Jesus spoke of an interesting responsibility of the Holy Ones. Both the rich man and Lazarus, the beggar, died. The rich man lifted up his eyes in Hades, being in torment. When Lazarus died, "he was carried away by the angels to Abraham's bosom . . . being comforted."[20] What an experience it must have been for Lazarus! And what a beautiful and comforting hope for the child of God—to be carried by angels into the presence of our wonderful Lord!

The well-known writer, Mrs. Hope B. Friedmann,

whose articles have appeared in many major Christian magazines, shares a heart-warming experience that came to her in an experience of bereavement.

"The summer had come, and with it a trip to the Northwest with six-year-old Sue. My three boys were boarding on a farm while their mother took a much needed rest with her parents.

"But my visit came to an abrupt end. After three idyllic days the phone rang. It was my husband's voice, full of concern. 'A polio epidemic has broken out in the city here. They have called me from the farm for Kent has difficulty swallowing, so I brought him to the hospital this morning. The doctor thinks possibly he has it.'

"Barely audible, I whispered, 'Is he paralyzed?'

" 'No. This is bulbar polio affecting centers in the brain. But, honey, try not to be overly worried for it may not be as bad as it seems. If his breathing becomes worse they will perform a tracheotomy and open his throat. I'll call you in the morning.'

"I replaced the receiver as if in a trance. Fear gripped me in tentacles of pain, anguish left me breathless. Eight-year-old Kent was alone. All I could do was walk the floor and pray. And at times I spoke to my parents.

" 'It doesn't look good,' my doctor-father said, and he put on his jacket, went outside, and started weeding his garden. Looking back, I know that not only were weeds pulled, but the flowers were watered with his tears.

"To wait and not to know was almost unbearable. The night hours were even harder to endure. I tossed, sleepless, in bed. My mind was in turmoil, torn with apprehension. What would tomorrow bring? Would the doctors operate? Would he have the best care? Was Kent suffering? frightened?

" 'Dear Lord,' I prayed, 'he is so small and I am so far away. Please help him not to feel alone. Help him understand somehow, that I will come first thing in the morning. God, help me to get there. I thought my faith in You was so strong, but I feel so helpless in this, so weak and needy, help me, help me!'

"Finally I slipped into the exhausted oblivion of sleep.

"Then, abruptly, I was awake. By my bed the luminous hands of the clock pointed to five. Grief and fear jolted me back to reality as the present settled over me in the early morning's grey darkness.

"Gradually I began to sense that I was no longer alone! A Presence was standing by my bed. A comforting warmth glowed into me. Peace surrounded me!

" 'What did he look like?' children ask me now, years later, when I tell them the story. 'Was the Presence bright like a Christmas angel? Was his face shining?' And I can only reply that his garments were soft, white and yet warm of color, that his face was obscure, that his voice was sure and gentle, and that I was not afraid.

"He bent over me and his words—I can never forget them—were distinct. 'I have taken care of everything and all is well. Do not worry.' Then as gently as he came, he vanished, leaving me quieted, pondering, and strangely at rest.

"Mother was busy, preparing breakfast when the

17

phone rang. With a finality akin to premonition, she stated, 'That must be the hospital calling you.' And it was.

" 'Kent died this morning at five, dearest.' My husband's toneless voice broke. This is only a dream, a nightmare from which I will awaken. Why, I countered, it was only a few days ago that I kissed his rosy cheek and waved my oldest and most vigorous child a merry goodbye. Dead? It was incredible!

"I hung up the phone, returned to the kitchen and sank into a chair.

"It must be true. Kent was really gone. It must be. His father had just said so. Kent had died this morning at five.

"At five. At five?

"I sat up, electrified!

"The time! The Presence! The words! 'I have taken care of everything and all is well. Do not worry!' Slowly it all came back. My mind began to clear and the quiet and peace his assurance had left with me returned and penetrated my grief. As I remembered, the meaning cleared, and with the comprehension came the strength I needed, and the assurance. I understood. Though I had not reached him in time, Kent had not been alone.

"I will always believe that as an angel appeared to Mary to say, 'Fear not,' and to the shepherds to announce, 'Behold, I bring you good tidings of great joy,' so also a Holy One came on another desolate night and bent low to say, 'All is well.'

"And as he bent low, a little boy and his mother found peace."

Looking again at that very significant first chapter

of Hebrews we discover that while the Holy Ones are greatly superior to man in glory, power and person, they are greatly inferior to Christ, the Son of God.

Christ Is the "Begotten Son"
While Angels Are Created Beings

While angels have names and rank, the Son's name excels them all. "He has inherited a more excellent name than they."[21] Michael, the archangel, is referred to by Daniel as "one of the chief princes" of the angelic order,[22] and both Daniel and Luke introduce to us the glorious Gabriel.[23] But the glory of these angelic names dims and fades in the ineffable radiance of that name which is above every name, and at which every knee shall bow and every tongue shall confess that He is Lord to the glory of God the Father.[24] Not of angels, but only of the name of the Begotten Son can it be said, "There is salvation in no one else; for there is no other name under heaven that has been given among men, by which we must be saved."[25]

Angels Are Inferior
to the Begotten Son in Worship

The greater is always worshiped by the lesser. And from the eternal God there came in ages past the command, "Let all the angels of God worship Him."[26] Instead of angels being objects of worship, they are subjects who worship Jesus Christ. Any worship, under any guise, of angels is wicked, idolatrous and forbidden. The apostle Paul warned, "Let no one keep defrauding you of your prize by delighting in self-abasement and the worship of angels, taking his stand on visions he has seen, inflated without cause by his fleshly mind, and not holding fast to the Head. . . ."[27]

Angels Are Inferior
to the Begotten Son in Authority

"But of the Son He says, 'Thy throne, O God, is forever and ever.' "[28] Peter emphasized this when he wrote of Christ, "who is at the right hand of God, having gone into heaven, after angels and authorities and powers had been subjected to Him."[29]

Yes, the time is coming when the "elders" of the angelic creation will fall down before the Lamb and to His glory will sing a new song. And what a song that will be!

"Worthy art Thou to take the book, and to break its seals; for Thou wast slain, and didst purchase for God with Thy blood men from every tribe and tongue and people and nation. And Thou hast made them to be a kingdom and priests to our God; and they will reign upon the earth."[30]

And then all the Holy Ones of the angel world—"all the angels . . . standing around the throne . . . and the number of them was myriads of myriads, and thousands of thousands"—will join in this refrain:

"Worthy is the Lamb that was slain to receive power and riches and wisdom and might and honor and glory and blessing."

As they sing, they will all fall down and worship the Begotten Son.[31] The angels will realize and rejoice in the fact that only He is worthy of worship for only He is King of kings and Lord of lords.

20

Footnotes to Chapter 2

1. Hebrews 1:5-14
2. Colossians 1:16
3. Matthew 22:30
4. Luke 20:36
5. Hebrews 1:14
6. Psalm 78:24,25
7. Genesis 18:1-8
8. Hebrews 13:2
9. Numbers 22:22-31
10. Judges 13:19,20
11. Daniel 3:25
12. 2 Peter 2:11
13. Psalm 103:20
14. Luke 9:26
15. Ezekiel 28:14-16
16. 2 Peter 2:4
17. Jude 6
18. 1 Peter 1:12
19. Matthew 24:36
20. Luke 16:19-31
21. Hebrews 1:4
22. Daniel 10:13
23. Daniel 8:16; 9:21; Luke 1:19,26
24. Philippians 2:9,10
25. Acts 4:12
26. Hebrews 1:6
27. Colossians 2:18,19
28. Hebrews 1:8
29. 1 Peter 3:22
30. Revelation 5:9,10
31. Revelation 5:11-14

CHAPTER 3

They Saw It Happen

The biblical account of creation is not confined to Genesis, the first book of the Bible. The words of Genesis 1:1 merely state the fact of creation: "In the beginning God created the heavens and the earth."

While the order of the creative acts is given in the verses that follow, nothing is revealed concerning the divine intent or plan nor is any information given regarding the reaction of creatures then living to this new creation of God. That other forms of life existed prior to the creation of the earth is evident from statements found throughout the Word of God.

We know that angels, the Holy Ones, were present when the Divine Architect laid the cornerstone and established the foundation of the earth. Many years ago a man by the name of Job became a bit too self-defensive and self-complimentary. Let's listen in as God interrogates him.

"Who is this that darkens counsel by words without knowledge? Now gird up your loins like a man, and I will ask you, and you instruct Me!

"Where were you when I laid the foundation of the earth! Tell Me, if you have understanding, who set its measurements, since you know? Or who stretched the line on it? On what were its bases sunk? Or who laid its cornerstone, when the morning stars sang together, and all the sons of God shouted for joy"?[1]

There can be no doubt that God was referring to angels when He spoke of "the sons of God." The same terminology is used in Job 1:6 and 2:1, ". . . There was a day when the sons of God came to present themselves before the Lord."

In these three references from the book of Job several facts about angels are revealed. Apparently the members of the angelic creation are required to report their activities to God on a regular basis. What is meant by "there was a day," we do not know. Nor do we know how frequently these reports are made, nor what all the angelic activities are. But one thing is certain. All members of the angelic creation, holy or fallen, are subject to the authority and will of Almighty God. He is Lord of all.

Another interesting fact revealed through the pen of this book's author is that the Holy Ones were present and witnessed the creation of this earth, and rejoiced in its creation. Angels are not subjects of time as we are. The writer of Hebrews reminds us that man was made lower than the angels.[2] The Holy Ones existed long before God breathed His breath of life into the form of clay and Adam became a living soul. And since angels do not die, they are timeless.

But the most significant information that God gives in His interrogation of Job is that when He made the earth "all the sons of God shouted for joy." Why did they rejoice? Were they ignorant of the fact that the curse of sin would blight the earth and its creatures? Did they not know that the creature made in the image of God would rebel against his benevolent Creator and become so depraved that "the wickedness of man was great on the earth, and that every intent of the thoughts of his heart was only evil continually"?[3]

Or did they rejoice because they were able to look down through the corridors of time to that moment when, outside the slumbering village of Bethlehem, they would again shout for joy?

Still another possible cause for the happiness displayed when the foundation of the earth was laid is suggested in Revelation 4:11. We are informed that all things were created by our Lord and our God for His pleasure. And if the creation of the earth brought pleasure to God, that in itself would cause the Holy Ones to shout together for joy.

All this may be true, but the most likely explanation for that heavenly praise meeting is to be found at Bethlehem of Judea. True, the Holy Ones "longed to look into" the redemptive truths of the new covenant and God's mystery of the ages, the Church, but were not permitted to fully understand or participate in it. But they did know something and it was so wonderful that heaven exploded with joy when the Christ child was born and laid in a manger.

The lone angel, who appeared to the shepherds with the thrilling announcement, "I bring you good news of a great joy which shall be for all the people; for today in the city of David there has been born for you a Savior, who is Christ the Lord," was soon joined by a multitude of the heavenly host—the Holy Ones. Then the shouts of joy that sounded through space when the earth was created were reechoed over the hills of Judea, "Glory to God in the highest, and on earth peace among men with whom He is pleased."[4]

But that is not the end of the creation story. The sons of God still shout for joy. Jesus told about it after relating the parables of the lost sheep and the lost coin. "I tell you, there is joy in the presence of the angels of God over one sinner who repents."[5]

Yes, unknown ages ago the Holy Ones shouted for joy as they celebrated the creation of this earth. More than nineteen hundred years ago the hills of Bethlehem were bathed in heavenly radiance as multitudes of the heavenly host joined in the festivity of the Saviour's birth. And today, as a lost soul is found by the Great Shepherd of the sheep and brought safely within God's fold, once again the sons of God shout for joy. There has been another creation—a new creation—a redeemed soul has been made a new creature in Christ Jesus. Old things have passed away and all things have become new! "Glory to God in the highest."

Footnotes to Chapter 3

1. Job 38:1-7
2. Hebrews 2:7
3. Genesis 6:5
4. Luke 2:14
5. Luke 15:10

CHAPTER 4

They Made It Happen

She was pregnant, but not by her own choice. A slave girl, she had little to say about her body or her future. She had been given as a concubine to Abraham by his wife, Sarai. And when she discovered that she was pregnant, can one blame her for the feeling of superiority she felt in relation to her barren mistress? Then the storm of ruthless abuse broke upon her as the jealous Sarai made every day a hell on earth for the luckless slave.

Finally, unable to take more abusive treatment, Hagar ran away. And there in the wilderness, by the spring on the road to Shur, Hagar had her first of two encounters with the Holy Ones. "The angel of the Lord found her. . . . and said to her, 'Return to your mistress, and submit yourself to her authority. . . . Behold, you are with child, and you shall bear a son; and you shall call his name Ishmael.' "[1]

About fifteen years later, Hagar again found herself in the desert, not a fugitive this time, but an outcast. In the distance, lying under a desert shrub, her son Ishmael was dying of thirst. And again came that voice, the one she had heard years before, "What is the matter with you, Hagar? Do not fear, for God has heard the voice of the lad where he is." Once again, it was "the angel of God" who called from heaven. "Then God opened her eyes and she saw a well of water; and she went and filled the skin with water, and gave the lad a drink. And God was with the lad."[2]

It is in this dramatic story we are introduced to angels in biblical history.

There is a previous mention of another order of heavenly beings. After Adam and Eve had rebelled against God's sovereignty, God "drove the man out; and at the east of the garden of Eden He stationed the cherubim, and the flaming sword which turned every direction, to guard the way to the tree of life."[3]

When King Hezekiah was threatened by Rabshakeh, general of the Assyrian army, he took the openly hostile and warning letter into the house of the Lord. There "he spread it out before the Lord. And Hezekiah prayed before the Lord and said, 'O Lord the God of Israel, who art enthroned above the cherubim, Thou art the God, Thou alone, of all the kingdoms of the earth. Thou hast made heaven and earth.' "[4]

In Ezekiel 10 a very detailed description of the cherubim is given. Here, as in Hezekiah's prayer, the throne of God is located over the cherubim. In Ezekiel's revelation of these mysterious heavenly creatures, they are described as having wings, with the

30

form of hands under their wings and flanked with
"wheels within wheels" which were "full of eyes all
around."

The cherubim apparently belong to the highest
order of heavenly being, occupying the position closest to the throne of God. In describing Lucifer and
his insurrection against God, Ezekiel identifies him
with the cherubim.

When Moses received instructions regarding the
construction of the Tabernacle and the Ark of the
Covenant, he was ordered to place two golden figures
of the cherubim on the cover of the ark. Cherubim
were also woven into the texture of the inner curtain
of the Tabernacle and the veil.

It is probable that the "living creatures" referred
to frequently in Revelation belonged to the cherubim
order.

In Isaiah 6, verse 2, is to be found the Bible's only
mention of still another form of heavenly life—the
six-winged seraphim. They are distinct from the
cherubim. In 1 Samuel 4:4, Psalm 80:1 and Psalm
99:1, God is said to be seated above the cherubim.
On the other hand, Isaiah saw the seraphim stand
above the Lord God. Apparently the duties of the
seraphim differ from those of the cherubim. The
cherubim seem to be the guardians of the throne of
God and God's ambassadors extraordinary. The
seraphim are concerned with the worship of God and
the purification of His servants for worship and service acceptable to God.

But as far as our common understanding of angels
is concerned, the cherubim and seraphim are not
angels. They belong to other forms of heavenly life.

probably higher ones, and there may be myriads of additional types of creatures in heaven.

Following Hagar's experiences with the Holy Ones, Abraham was the next person to have an encounter with an angel.

The altar had been built, the wood was placed upon it and the sacrifice was bound and lifted upon the wood. The mountain-top breeze fanned the burning coals in the brazen censer as it stood upon a nearby rock. The old man raised the knife to plunge it into the heart of the sacrifice victim, grief such as seldom seen on earth was pictured in his face. Tears streamed from his eyes and trickled down his white beard.

And then it happened! "Abraham, Abraham!" The knife was stayed in midair! The old man's startled gaze swept over the mountain top and then lifted toward heaven. He had heard that voice before.

"Here I am."

"Do not stretch out your hand against the lad, and do nothing to him; for now I know that you fear God, since you have not withheld your son, your only son, from Me."[5]

Whose voice was it? "The angel of the Lord called to him from heaven." Many Bible scholars believe the "angel of the Lord" was a pre-incarnate revelation of the Son of God, not a messenger sent from God, but a theophany.

Going further into biblical history, one would hardly expect one of the Holy Ones to act in the capacity of cupid. But it did happen!

When Abraham sent his trusted servant Eliezer to seek a bride for his son, Isaac, he assured the servant,

"The Lord, the God of heaven, who took me from my father's house and from the land of my birth, and who spoke to me, and who swore to me, saying, 'To your descendants I will give this land,' He will send His angel before you, and you will take a wife for my son from there."⁶ And the angel *did* go before Eliezer and did a beautiful job in arranging a wonderful romance for Isaac.

Lot, the nephew of Abraham, had an experience with angels that brought both deliverance and tragedy. Two angels arrived at his home in Sodom one evening. The men of the community attempted to seize them and rape them. The angels smote the men with blindness and ordered Lot to take his family and flee from wicked Sodom. As they fled, Lot's wife disobeyed the command of the angels and looked back. Instantly she became a pillar of salt! Lot and his two unmarried daughters were saved from the fiery destruction of Sodom and Gomorrah.⁷ The angels who brought salvation to Lot were the ones who brought destruction and death to the inhabitants of the cities of the valley. Herein we can see that the Holy Ones are God's messengers of destruction and they also serve as God's messengers of deliverance.

Jacob, the son of Isaac, had a very interesting history and much of it was not commendable. He cheated his brother Esau; he deceived his blind father; by trickery he took over all his uncle Laban's possessions; but he met God at the brook Jabbok and his character was transformed. Jacob the cheat became Israel the Prince—he who had power with God and with man.⁸

During the course of his checkered career, Jacob had several encounters with angels. While fleeing from the murderous wrath of his brother, Esau, "he came to a certain place and spent the night there, because the sun had set; and he took one of the stones of the place and put it under his head, and lay down in that place.

"And he had a dream, and behold, a ladder was set on the earth with its top reaching to heaven; and behold, the angels of God were ascending and descending on it. . . . Then Jacob awoke from his sleep and said 'Surely the Lord is in this place, and I did not know it'."[9]

As Jacob neared the end of his life, looking back over his many experiences, realizing what an important part the Holy Ones had played in his life, he exclaimed, "God . . . has been my shepherd all my life to this day, the angel who has redeemed me from all evil."[10]

Many years later as the children of Israel faced the formidable task of conquering the mighty nations of Canaan and possessing their lands, the Lord God Jehovah assured Moses that there was nothing to fear. He said, "Behold, I am going to send an angel before you to guard you along the way, and to bring you into the place which I have prepared. . . . for My angel will go before you and bring you in to the land."[11] And that bringing "in to the land" process had actually started more than forty years before when the mighty Pharaoh refused to release the Israelites from bondage. Recalling that experience, Moses wrote, "But when we cried out to the Lord, He heard our voice and sent an angel and brought us out of Egypt."[12] Nor did the Holy One assigned to the deliverance of Israel forsake them after their emancipation from Egypt. As they were passing through the Red Sea, which had been miraculously divided, they were pursued by the armies of Egypt. Then "the angel of God, who had been going before the camp of Israel, moved and went behind them; and the pillar of cloud moved from before them and stood behind them. So it came between the camp of Egypt and the camp of Israel; and there was the cloud along with the darkness, yet it gave light at night. Thus the one did not come near the other all night."[13]

Much later, one of the great prophets of Israel had an interesting experience with an angel. Elijah had fearlessly challenged the prophets of Baal to a showdown. The losers would die! The prophets of Baal erected their altar and placed a bullock upon it. Then they called upon their god, Baal, to send fire to consume their sacrifice. As evening drew near. Elijah erected an altar, placed his sacrifice upon it. dug a trench about it and then drenched the sacrifice and the wood and filled the trench with water. In a simple prayer of faith the prophet asked Jehovah to answer with fire. A sheet of flame shot into the air from Elijah's altar, consuming the sacrifice, the wood, the water and even the stones and the dust about the altar![14] The prophets of Baal were seized and slain by the brook Kishon. In those days, they played for keeps. What a victory for the prophet of God! And then the rain came—buckets of it—after years of drought!

And it was then, at the moment of his greatest

victory, that the prophet failed. The wicked queen Jezebel sent word to Elijah that she would kill him just as he had slain her prophets of Baal, and the prophet fled for his life. A victim of self-pity, he prayed, "It is enough; now, O Lord, take my life, for I am not better than my fathers." And then he slept. He was awakened by a touch—the touch of an angel—an angel who also served as his cook! "Arise, eat."

"Then he looked and behold, there was at his head a bread cake baked on hot stones, and a jar of water. So he ate and drank and lay down again. And the angel of the Lord came again a second time and touched him and said, 'Arise, eat, because the journey is too great for you.' So he arose and ate and drank, and went in the strength of that food forty days and forty nights to Horeb, the mountain of God."[15] For God's distraught, discouraged and exhausted prophet the Holy One provided super vitamins that kept him going for forty days!

Then, there is that exciting story of Daniel in the lions' den. He was a man of prayer and a man of courage. And what a testimony he had from a pagan king! As the moment of truth approached and Daniel was about to be thrown to the lions, King Darius said to him, "Your God whom you constantly serve will Himself deliver you." After a sleepless night the king approached the den and cried out with a troubled voice, "Daniel, servant of the living God, has your God, whom you constantly serve, been able to deliver you from the lions?" Someone had gone into that lions' den before Daniel did. It was an angel! And Daniel was able to answer the king, "O king, live forever! My God sent His angel and shut the lions' mouths, and they have not harmed me."[16]

We are indebted to one of the Holy Ones for that important prophetic book of Zechariah. God used an angel to inform the prophet of many of the most important prophetic events, some of which are now history, and many of which are yet to be fulfilled.

The prophet wrote, "I saw at night, and behold, a man was riding on a red horse, and he was standing among the myrtle trees which were in the ravine, with red, sorrel, and white horses behind him. Then I said, 'My lord, what are these?' And the angel who was speaking with me said to me, 'I will show you what these are'."[17]

The angel then proceeded to reveal to Zechariah a marvelous insight into the organized activities of the earth department of the angelic order. There were angels who patrolled the earth and reported earth conditions to God. Other angels had the responsibility of scattering the people of Judah. Still others were sent to punish those nations which had overreacted against the Israelites. Some angels were, and undoubtedly are, preparing the way for the regathering of the Jews and the restoration of the glory of the Davidic kingdom. Chapter after chapter of this interesting book is devoted to angelic responsibilities.

Nor is angelic activity confined to Old Testament history. In fact, we receive much more information about the Holy Ones from the New Testament than is to be found in all the books of the Old Testament. Presently, we will look at only one of these instances.

Herod's murder of James had so pleased the Jewish people that the king decided to make them even happier by executing Peter. So Peter was arrested and Herod "put him in prison, delivering him to four squads of soldiers to guard him, intending after the Passover to bring him out before the people. So Peter was kept in the prison, but prayer for him was being made fervently by the church to God.

"And on the very night when Herod was about to bring him forward, Peter was sleeping between two soldiers, bound with two chains; and guards in front of the doors were watching over the prison.

"And behold, an angel of the Lord suddenly appeared, and a light shone in the cell; and he struck Peter's side and roused him, saying, 'Get up quickly.' And his chains fell off his hands. And the angel said to him, 'Gird yourself and put on your sandals.' And he did so. And he said to him, 'Wrap your cloak around you and follow me.' And he went out and continued to follow, and he did not know that what was being done by the angel was real, but thought he was seeing a vision. . . . And when Peter came to himself, he said, 'Now I know for sure that the Lord has sent forth His angel and rescued me from the hand of Herod and from all that the Jewish people were expecting.' "[18]

This rapid glance through biblical history reveals much of the activities and concerns of the Holy Ones. To Hagar, the slave girl, the angel brought comfort and also demanded submission. In their later encounter, the angel gave assurance and life-sustaining water to the young mother and her son Ishmael, and then promised to them a divine covenant of prosperity and blessing.

The angel who stayed the knife of Abraham saved

the life of Isaac and rewarded him for his remarkable faith and obedience by returning his beloved son safe and sound. The angel understood the pathos of a father's heart.

The Holy One who accompanied Abraham's servant, Eliezer, took the responsibility of securing a lovely bride for the lonely Isaac. And who can deny that what the angel whispered in the ear of the damsel Rebekah had a great deal to do with her decision and her reply to the question, "Will you go with this man? And she said, 'I will go.' " Perhaps eternity will reveal that many wonderful Christian romances were actually made in heaven—that the meeting of the boy and the girl was not by accident—that it was a rendezvous arranged by one of the Holy Ones.

It is significant that although Lot, Abraham's nephew, had drifted far from the holy standards of his uncle and had sought the companionship and material benefits of an unholy alliance, yet the angels of the Lord were there to spare his life and assist him in avoiding the consequences of his own poor judgment.

What a story of grace is to be found in Jacob's encounter with one of the Holy Ones. Certainly no one was less deserving of a fresh start, with a new name and a new character, but it happened! And when we wander from the will of God and fail and fail again, those circumstances or words which brought us back may well have been of angelic origin.

And a wonderful thing about the angels of history, and the angels of today, is that they understand us—our weaknesses and our needs, our fears and our foolishness. They meet us where we are and minister to us. When Elijah was wishing he could die, the angel didn't tell him to pray and confess his sin. He made two hot meals for him and gave him a cool refreshing drink. As for Daniel, the Holy One knew just what Daniel needed, so he gave all the lions a temporary infection of lockjaw and to the prophet a good night's rest.

Perhaps no angelic ministry of history better illustrates the tender concern of these Holy Ones for God's children than does Peter's experience when he had been imprisoned by Herod. Notice the procedure of deliverance. The galling chains were made to fall from Peter's wrists. Then the angel said, "Get dressed, Peter." Then he added, "Put your sandals on, I don't want you to catch cold." And finally, "Now, Peter, wrap your cloak around you, it's quite chilly out tonight." When a Holy One arranges a jail break, he takes care of all the details involved in the safety and health of the delivered one.

It is important for us to remember that God is not only the God of history and prophecy, but also the God of today. The Holy Ones who opened the prison doors for Peter's deliverance are actively engaged in bringing deliverance here and now to the heirs of salvation.

In her book, *Marching Orders for the End Battle,*[19] Corrie ten Boom tells how, during the Jeunesse rebellion in the Congo, "when the rebels advanced on a school where two hundred children of missionaries lived, they planned to kill both children and teachers. In the school they knew of the danger and therefore went to prayer. Their only protection was a fence and a couple of soldiers, while the enemy, who came closer and closer, amounted to several hundreds. When the rebels were close by, suddenly something happened: they turned around and ran away! The next day the same thing happened and again on the third day. One of the rebels was wounded and was brought to the mission hospital. When the doctor was busy dressing his wounds, he asked him: 'Why did you not break into the school as you planned?' 'We could not do it. We saw hundreds of soldiers in white uniforms and we became scared.' In Africa soldiers never wear white uniforms, so it must have been angels!"

How great is our God! How loving is our heavenly Father and how tender and thoughtful are the "ministering spirits (who) are sent out to render service for the sake of those who will inherit salvation!"

Footnotes to Chapter 4
1. Genesis 16:1-11
2. Genesis 21:14-20
3. Genesis 3:24
4. 2 Kings 19:14,15
5. Genesis 22:1-13
6. Genesis 24:7
7. Genesis 19
8. Genesis 32
9. Genesis 28:11-16

10. Genesis 48:15,16
11. Exodus 23:20,23
12. Numbers 20:16
13. Exodus 14:19,20
14. 1 Kings 18:30-40
15. 1 Kings 19:1-8
16. Daniel 6:16-23
17. Zechariah 1:8,9
18. Acts 12:1-11
19. Corrie ten Boom, *Marching Orders for the End Battle* (Fort Washington, Pa.: Christian Literature Crusade, London, 1969), p. 88.

CHAPTER 5

Heaven's "Special Delivery Service"

One of the most common responsibilities of the Holy Ones is stated in the fourteenth verse of the first chapter of Hebrews where they are referred to as those who are "sent out." This seems to be particularly true of their activities as recorded in the Old Testament. They were God's "Special Delivery" messengers.

To Abraham the Holy Ones revealed the impending destruction of the cities of the plain. And it was the delivery of this communication which prompted that remarkable and somewhat humorous intercession on the part of Abraham: "Suppose there are fifty . . . ? forty-five? . . . forty? . . . thirty? . . . twenty? . . . Suppose ten are found there?" Would the Lord spare the whole place on their account?[1]

A Holy One was sent to the wife of Manoah with the message that she would give birth to a son who would deliver Israel from the Philistines. "Then the angel of the Lord appeared to the woman, and said to her, 'Behold now, you are barren and have borne no children, but you shall conceive and give birth to a son . . . and no razor shall come upon his head, for the boy shall be a Nazirite to God from the womb; and he shall begin to deliver Israel from the hands of the Philistines."[2] An unusual feature of this incident is that, in answer to the prayer of Manoah, the angel returned to reiterate the message previously given to his wife. This suggests the fascinating possibility that we may, with success, when circumstances would justify it, ask for a visitation from one of the Holy Ones.

In the book of Daniel we find recorded several "Special Deliveries" by angels. "Belshazzar the king held a great feast for a thousand of his nobles, and he was drinking wine in the presence of the thousand. . . . they brought the gold vessels that had been taken out of the temple, the house of God which was in Jerusalem; and the king and his nobles, his wives, and his concubines drank from them. They drank the wine and praised the gods of gold and silver, of bronze, iron, wood and stone.

"Suddenly the fingers of a man's hand emerged and began writing opposite the lampstand on the plaster of the king's palace, and the king saw the back of the hand that did the writing. . . . Now this is the inscription that was written out: 'MENE, MENE, TEKEL, UPHARSIN.'

"This is the interpretation of the message:

" 'MENE'—God has numbered your kingdom and put an end to it.

" 'TEKEL'—You have been weighed on the scales and found deficient.

" 'PERES'—your kingdom has been divided and given to the Medes and Persians.

". . . That same night Belshazzar the Chaldean king was slain."[3]

Whose hand wrote that fateful prediction on the wall of the palace? Daniel told Belshazzar that "the hand was sent from . . . the God in whose hand are your life-breath and your ways." There can be no doubt that it was the hand of a Holy One that traced those words upon the plaster!

Some years later, Daniel said he was "speaking and praying, and confessing my sin and the sin of my people Israel, and presenting my supplication before the Lord my God . . . while I was still speaking in prayer, then the man Gabriel . . . came to me in my extreme weariness about the time of the evening offering.

"And he gave me instruction and talked with me, and said, 'O Daniel, I have now come forth to give you insight with understanding. At the beginning of your supplications the command was issued, and I have come to tell you, for you are highly esteemed; so give heed to the message and gain understanding of the vision.' "[4]

Then follows the most detailed and amazing prophecies to be found in the Bible! And they came to Daniel through the "Special Delivery Service" of the Holy Ones referred to in Daniel 8:13.

For four hundred years there had been neither message nor prophet. God was silent. Then the "Fulness of time" approached. A godly priest was ministering in the Temple when ". . . an angel of the Lord appeared to him, standing to the right of the altar of incense. And Zacharias was troubled when he saw him, and fear gripped him.

"But the angel said to him, 'Do not be afraid, Zacharias, for your petition has been heard, and your wife Elizabeth will bear you a son, and you will give him the name John. . . . And it is he who will go as a forerunner before Him in the spirit and power of Elijah, to turn the hearts of the fathers back to the children, and the disobedient to the attitude of the righteous; so as to make ready a people prepared for the Lord.' "[5]

With this "Special Delivery" by one of the Holy Ones, the wheels of redemption were set in motion and eventuated in Calvary, the empty tomb and every agent and agency involved today in the fulfillment of the Great Commission.

Five months after Zacharias' encounter with the angel, the same Holy One, Gabriel, delivered a message to a lovely and deeply spiritual girl living in the obscure village of Bethlehem. And what a "Special Delivery" that was! For millenniums, numberless women had hoped and prayed that God would choose them to mother the promised Messiah. Now the time had come and Gabriel received the message and was ordered to deliver it to Mary of Bethlehem.

"And coming in, he said to her, 'Hail, favored one! The Lord is with you.' But she was greatly troubled at this statement, and kept pondering what kind of salutation this might be.

"And the angel said to her, 'Do not be afraid, Mary; for you have found favor with God. And behold, you will conceive in your womb, and bear a son, and you shall name Him Jesus. He will be great, and will be called the Son of the Most High; and the Lord God will give Him the throne of His Father

David; and He will reign over the house of Jacob forever; and His kingdom will have no end.' "[6]

Some months later when Mary's pregnancy became obvious, the delivery service was again pressed into action. "Mary . . . was found to be with child by the Holy Spirit. And Joseph, her husband, being a righteous man, and not wanting to disgrace her, desired to put her away secretly. But when he had considered this, behold, an angel of the Lord appeared to him in a dream, saying, 'Joseph, son of David, do not be afraid to take Mary as your wife; for that which has been conceived in her is of the Holy Spirit. And she will bear a Son; and you shall call His name Jesus, for it is He who will save His people from their sins.' "[7]

Yes, it was a Holy One who first brought that sweet, wonderful name of God's Son to a human ear. I wonder which angel was chosen for this great honor? Could it have been Gabriel again?

After the Child had been born and His life was threatened by the jealous Herod, again using the vehicle of a dream, "an angel of the Lord appeared to Joseph in a dream, saying, 'Arise and take the Child and His mother, and flee to Egypt, and remain there until I tell you; for Herod is going to search for the Child to destroy Him.' " And some time later, "when Herod was dead, behold, an angel of the Lord appeared in a dream to Joseph in Egypt, saying, 'Arise and take the Child and His mother, and go into the land of Israel; for those who sought the Child's life are dead.' "[8]

Heaven's "Special Delivery Service" has been used through the ages to deliver divine telegrams of deliverance from death, birth notices, warnings of impending judgment, prophetic previews of future incidents and ages, and then, the greatest of all heaven's telegrams, "Unto you is born . . . a Saviour which is Christ the Lord."

In moments of danger, when escape from disaster is humanly impossible, more frequently than we realize, the heavenly messengers are sent on their missions of deliverance. The late Dr. A. C. Gaebelein, in his book, *The Angels of God*, tells of divine intervention in his behalf.

"A number of years ago, while traveling northward, we committed ourselves especially into His loving hands. There was a feeling of danger in the heart. The Lord gave a night of peaceful rest. But in the morning we heard the story of what had happened during the night. The train was hours late and the crew told us that near to midnight the train had been flagged by a farmer and had been brought to a stop less than five yards from a deep abyss. A storm further north sent its flood-waters down the creek and washed the wooden bridge away. The farmer was asleep. He said a voice awoke him to arise. He heard the rushing water and hastily dressed himself and lit a lantern, when he heard the oncoming train, which he stopped in time. We have always believed that an angel of God acted then."[9]

There is no reason to believe that God has discontinued His "Special Delivery Service." In times of discouragement and testing, when we have exhausted our store of endurance, there is every possibility that we may be visited by one of the Holy Ones.

In a heart-warming story which first appeared in

the *Wheaton College Bulletin*,[10] the late Dr. V. Raymond Edman said: "On life's pathway we today may meet angels. I mean that literally and not metaphorically. We know and love godly and gracious friends and relatives whom we sometimes describe as 'angels,' and yet we know they are human beings whose kindness and graciousness reveal the indwelling Saviour. Beyond every human consideration, I am persuaded from the Scriptures that angels are present in this world. Usually they are unseen by human eyes, and yet their service can be very real to the Christian who is 'an heir of salvation.' Sometimes their service requires appearance in human form, and nothing about their dress or speech would make them different from those who are present. Only the discerning heart understands, and that usually long afterward, that the stranger who helped at a moment of great emergency was in reality one of God's angels.

"Mrs. Edman and I were young missionaries in the Andean highlands of the lovely little republic of Ecuador in western South America. After our marriage in the capital city of Quito, we were given our first assignment to a city whose environs had thousands of Quichua-speaking Indians. We lived on the outskirts of that city where we could reach both the Spanish-speaking citizens on the streets and in the marketplaces, and also the shy, suspicious Indians who passed our doorway on the way to market.

"Our assignment was a difficult one. The people were quite unfriendly, and some were fanatical in their bitter opposition to our presence in their city. On occasion small crowds would gather to hurl insults, punctuated by stones, both large and small. Now and then school children would parade in the dusty street before our home and repeat what they had been taught to say against us. The Indians from the countryside were especially timid about having any friendly contact with us because of intimidation by some of the townspeople. As a result it was often difficult to get the bare necessities of life—fruits and vegetables, or charcoal for the kitchen stove.

"Added to these physical factors was an inward sense of human loneliness. There was never fear, but one was aware that there were very few who in the remotest sense were the least friendly.

"Let me describe the little home we had rented. Perhaps a brief sketch of its environs will help. Across the front of the lot was the usual high iron fence with its large gate of grillwork. Then there was a small garden with flowers and a little fountain. Then came the house about a half-story higher than the garden.

"Whenever we were not in the front part of the house we kept the gate locked with an iron chain and a great padlock. There was constant danger that some bare-footed stranger would tiptoe into an unoccupied room and depart with more than that with which he had entered. The gate had to be locked securely at night, of course, and the same was true when we had our meals.

"One noon as we were eating we heard a rattling on the gate as though someone were asking for admission. I excused myself from the table and went to the porch. Then I saw an Indian woman standing outside the gate. She had reached one hand inside through the bars and was knocking on the chain with the padlock. Quickly I went down to inquire what she might want. She was no one I had ever seen before, and the small bundle she carried on her shoulder did not indicate that she had any vegetables to offer for sale.

"As I approached the inside of the gate she began to speak softly, in the mixture of Spanish and Quichua that was typical of the Indians who lived fairly close to the town. Pointing to a gospel verse we had put on the porch she inquired, 'Are you the people who have come to tell us about the living God?'

"Her question startled me. No one had ever made that query before. Therefore, with surprise, I answered, *Mamita* (Little mother, the customary term for a woman of her years), yes we are.'

"Then she raised the hand that was still inside the locked gate, and began to pray. I still can see that hand and arm with its beads, in typical Indian style. She wore the heavy hat of the mountain woman. She had a small bundle and the typical blue shawl over her shoulders. She wore the white homespun waist with its primitive embroidery, and her dress was *balleta* (coarse woolen cloth) with a brightly colored homemade belt. Of course, she was barefooted.

"She prayed for the blessing of God upon the inhabitants of this home. She asked that we have courage for the service committed to us, that we have joy in doing God's bidding, and prayed that many would hear and obey the words of the gospel. Then she pronounced a blessing from God upon me.

"The prayer concluded, she withdrew her hand. Then she smiled at me through the gate with a final,

51

Dios le bendiga, 'God bless you.' Her eyes fairly shone as she spoke those words, and then she bowed and turned to her left.

"I was so astonished by all of this that for part of a minute I stood speechless and motionless. Quickly I remembered that it was the heat of the day, and that she should come in and eat with us. All the while I had held the key in my hand. In a matter of seconds I had unlocked the gate and stepped out to call her back. She could not have gone more than five or ten yards.

"But she was not there! Where could she have gone so quickly? It was at least fifty yards from our gate to the corner of the street, and there was no gate along that stretch of wall, either on our side of the street or across the way.

"I ran to the corner with the persuasion that if it had been possible for her to have reached that far then certainly she would be right there. Immediately I looked to the right but she was not there. As I ran to the corner I could look down our street for nearly half a mile, and there were no openings in the wall in that direction. On both sides were large corrals. The same was true of the street to my left.

"Where could she be? The closest gate was to my right and that nearly a block away. There I ran (and my days on the track team in school stood me in good stead at the age of twenty-four). I rushed inside the open gate and there were my two closest neighbors, repairing the spokes in a large wooden wheel. Hastily I inquired, 'Did an Indian woman just come in here?'

"Both men looked up at once from their work and replied, 'No, sir.'

" 'I mean just now,' I insisted.

" 'No, sir, we have been right here in the gate for an hour or more, and nobody has entered or left during that time.'

"I thanked them, and hastened back to the corner. There was not a soul in sight.

"She must be somewhere; but where could she have gone? I waited there nearly ten minutes looking in all directions, but no one appeared on the street. Slowly I retraced my steps to my own gate, and after locking it again went back to the table.

" 'Where have you been so long?' inquired Friend Wife.

" 'There was an elderly Indian woman knocking on the gate. She prayed for us and invoked God's blessing upon us and then started on down the street. I unlocked the gate and stepped out to call her, but she was not along the wall as I had expected. So I ran to the corner and sought her, but in vain.'

" 'Strange!'

"We spoke no more about the matter. However, for days afterward my own heart remained strangely moved. It burned within me as I recalled the Indian woman's prayer, and it was strengthened by the blessing she had pronounced upon me. There seemed to be an aroma indescribably sweet and indefinable which certainly did not come from the flowers in the garden.

"After some days, I began to reflect upon that word in Hebrews 13:2, 'Be not forgetful to entertain strangers; for thereby some have entertained angels unawares.' I began to understand that the Almighty had none of His earthly servants at hand to encourage two young missionaries, so He was pleased to send an angel from heaven."

Yes, the Holy Ones are alive and they are here on earth! They are concerned about you as a child of God, and they are caring for you. It is entirely possible that one of these days, as you are entertaining a stranger, you will hear him say, "Special Delivery—it's from heaven!"

Footnotes to Chapter 5

1. Genesis 18:17-33
2. Judges 13:3-5
3. Daniel 5:1-30
4. Daniel 9:20-23
5. Luke 1:11-17
6. Luke 1:28-33
7. Matthew 1:18-21
8. Matthew 2:13,19,20
9. Gaebelein, Arno Clemens, *The Angels of God* (Publication Office "Our Hope").
10. Wheaton College Bulletin, December, 1959.

CHAPTER 6

Angels in Evangelism

The most important task the Christian church faces today is the fulfillment of the Great Commission. God always has been, and is today, willing that none should perish but that all should come to repentance. Jesus Christ commanded us to pray the Lord of the harvest that He would thrust forth laborers into His harvest. Since God so loved the world that He gave His only begotten Son for it—since Christ came to seek and to save that which was lost—it is logical to conclude that the evangelization of the world has top priority on the divine schedule.

The apostle Paul said that the ministry of reconciliation, whereby men are reconciled to God, has been committed to us—to men and women—to those who themselves have been reconciled to God by the death of His Son.[1]

The question we will be considering in this chapter is, "Do the Holy Ones have any part whatever in this crucial ministry of determining human destinies through evangelism?"

Accepting the definition of evangelism as "the telling of the good news," it is subsequently very significant that the ministry of evangelism was first introduced to the world by the Holy Ones. It was an angel who said to the shepherds, "I bring you good news of a great joy which shall be for all the people; for today in the city of David there has been born for you a Savior, who is Christ the Lord."[2]

It was an angel of the Lord who gave the name of evangelism to Joseph, ". . . she will bear a Son; and you shall call His name Jesus, for it is He who will save His people from their sins."[3]

Following the death of the Lord Jesus Christ, when the women came to the tomb early on the first day of the week, it was one of the Holy Ones who first stated that cardinal doctrine of the Christian faith, the keystone distinctive of Christian evangelism, "He has risen, just as He said."[4] And it was that same angel who gave the first commission of evangelism: "Go quickly and tell. . . ."[5]

Lest we conclude that the participation of the Holy Ones in the ministry of evangelism was no longer necessary after the personal coming of the Holy Spirit, Scriptures call our attention to *increased* angelic activity *after* Pentecost.

Philip had enjoyed tremendous success at Samaria. ". . . Multitudes with one accord were giving attention to what was said by Philip, as they heard and saw the signs which he was performing. . . . When they believed Philip preaching the good news about the kingdom of God and the name of Jesus Christ, they were . . . baptized, men and women alike."[6]

Probably Philip was looking forward to many

happy months of fellowship with these precious children in the faith. But God had other plans for Philip. There were other sheep—at least one sheep—of another fold which had to be brought into *the* fold. So, ". . . an angel of the Lord spoke to Philip saying, 'Arise and go south to the road that descends from Jerusalem to Gaza.' (This is a desert road.)"[7]

God knew where Philip was most needed and He used one of His Holy Ones to thrust the evangelist into a new area of evangelism.

The next activity of angels in the field of evangelism came as quite a surprise to the Jerusalem church. Philip's successful evangelistic campaign at Samaria shocked the Jewish Christian community. After all, "Jews have no dealings with Samaritans." But the Holy Spirit recognizes no racial barriers, then or now.

Then something incredible happened!

"There was a certain man at Caesarea named Cornelius . . . a devout man, and one who feared God with all his household, and gave many alms to the Jewish people, and prayed to God continually. About the ninth hour of the day he clearly saw in a vision an angel of God who had just come to him, and said to him, 'Cornelius!' And fixing his gaze upon him and being much alarmed, he said, 'What is it, Lord?' And he said to him, 'Your prayers and alms have ascended as a memorial before God. And now dispatch some men to Joppa, and send for a man named Simon, who is also called Peter; he is staying with a certain tanner named Simon, whose house is by the sea.' "[8]

It is not surprising that an angel would come to a man like Cornelius. After all, he was a good man:

fearing God, praying, giving generously. No one deserved a heavenly visit more than he did. But there was a problem. He was not a Jew. But he was to be the door to a new field of evangelism, a door that had to be opened if it is true that God loved "all the world." And it was a Holy One who turned the knob to open that door!

Malcolm Hunter, missionary to Ethiopia, tells of a modern "Cornelius."

"One young Wallamo man heard the gospel message from one of our missionaries, believed it and decided to serve this new God. But he was so poor that he could not support his family so he decided to travel south to seek employment. At the end of twelve months he received his year's wages which amounted to the princely sum of nine Ethiopian dollars. Wishing to earn a little more, he traveled even further south and crossed into Gamu territory, where he was accosted by a local chieftain who relieved him of his hard-earned dollars.

"The Wallamo, bruised, penniless, and miles from home, muttered bitterly to himself, 'That God I have been worshiping is no good. If He is powerful He would have stopped that chief from stealing my money. I'll find a witch doctor and get him to put a curse on that chief and make him return my money.'

"The local witch doctor was said to be very powerful and to have put very many curses and spells on cattle and people and he was feared for miles around.

"As the Wallamo entered the gloomy hut of the witch doctor, suddenly a brilliant light appeared on the floor! He thought it was something caused through the power of the witch doctor, but the witch doctor believed it came from his visitor.

" 'Who is your god?' said the witch doctor in awed tones. 'He must be very powerful.'

"Bewildered and confused, the Wallamo stammered, 'I have been worshiping a new God, but He is no good. I am going back to the old ways. I want you to curse a man who robbed me.'

" 'Tell me what happened.'

"Briefly the Wallamo recounted what had befallen him, then was utterly amazed to hear this fearsome looking follower of Satan say, 'Your God is punishing you because all you thought about was money. You ought not to have left your family. Go back to them at once, but first tell me all you know about this new God.'

"Haltingly, the Wallamo told all that he could remember hearing from the missionaries. Then he set off to return home, while the witch doctor, although he had heard so little, believed, and went about telling his people that they must stop worshiping Satan and turn to the Great God of heaven.

"For a time people thought he had gone crazy, but were too afraid to oppose him openly.

"Then one night as he slept he had a vision, and in it he heard an angelic being say, 'I have been sent from the Great God because He has heard your prayers. You must go north to a village which is four days' walk from here, and there you will hear more about this God you are trying to serve.'

"As soon as it was light the man started on his long journey, living mostly on roots and berries. After four days, he reached the place mentioned by the angel—a place he had never heard of previously. There he found a small mission station and eagerly he listened to all the missionaries could tell him about God and His Son Jesus Christ.

"For several weeks he drank in all that was told him, then longing to share this wonderful news with his own people he returned home and began to teach and preach. For a time he suffered persecution and rejection, but gradually first one then another began to believe, and in time a small church was established with this one-time witch doctor as its pastor."

In a letter to his parents, Dr. and Mrs. John Hunter, Malcolm wrote, "That church was the one Jean and I visited one wet Sunday morning, and it was in the home of the ex-witch doctor that we were warmed and fed, and where we sat spellbound listening to his story. He is an old man now, frail and often sick, but a living testimony to the fact that, as in the case of Cornelius, God knew the desires of his heart, and chose him to be an instrument of blessing in that stronghold of Satan."

No human instrument has been so greatly used of God in the field of evangelism as was the apostle Paul. And when God uses a man, Satan will attempt to remove him. If he cannot accomplish his evil design through temptation, he will seek to kill him.

So widely and so effectively had Paul proclaimed Christ that he was able to say that all who dwelt in Asia had heard the gospel.

Then Paul was arrested and the Devil attempted to shut Paul's mouth by confining him in prison. But Paul, as a Roman citizen, appealed to Caesar, and the governor, Festus, had no choice but to acquiesce.

So Paul sailed for Rome. Then the northeaster caught the ship in midsea. Recalling that storm, Luke wrote, "Since neither sun nor stars appeared for many days, and no small storm was assailing us, from then on all hope of our being saved was gradually abandoned."[9] It appeared that Satan would be successful and Paul would be lost to the ministry of evangelism.

Then heaven moved into action. God summoned one of the Holy Ones and ordered that he deliver a message to His evangelist.

Standing on the heaving decks of the sinking vessel, Paul told the crew of the message he had received from heaven. "This very night an angel of the God to whom I belong and whom I serve stood before me, saying, 'Do not be afraid, Paul; you must stand before Caesar; and behold, God has granted you all those who are sailing with you.' Therefore, keep up your courage, men, for I believe God, that it will turn out exactly as I have been told."[10]

Encouraged and sustained by this visit from the Holy One, Paul went on to Rome and to an ever-widening ministry of evangelism through his epistles.

There are many indications that we are approaching the end of the end times. The coming of the Lord is drawing nigh. One of these days the Lord Himself will descend from heaven with a shout and we shall meet the Lord in the air and be forever with Him. The world will then pass through the catastrophic days of the Great Tribulation, but even so, the Holy Ones will be involved in the sacred task of evangelism. There is no statement nor inference anywhere in the Bible to support the popular belief that the Jewish remnant—the sealed 144,000—will go forth to evangelize the world during the dark days of the Tribulation. But the world will be evangelized, and by a Holy One.

Looking with prophetic vision down through the corridors of time, the apostle John described what he saw. "I saw another angel flying in midheaven, having an eternal gospel to preach to those who live on the earth, and to every nation and tribe and tongue and people; and He said with a loud voice, 'Fear God, and give Him glory, because the hour of His judgment has come; and worship Him who made the heaven and the earth and the sea and springs of waters.' "[11]

In all these biblical references we see that angels have been involved in evangelism both prophetically and historically. But they also are involved in contemporary evangelism.

Mr. Dan Peters, an advertising executive of Glendale, California, relates a personal incident.

"A recent hire in my department was a very withdrawn man, very far out in clothes and appearance and his total character was somewhat strange. One morning his wife called my office and asked if he had reported for work. He had not shown up at the house the night before, nor at work the following morning. As I questioned his associates, I found that he had been hitting the petty cash frequently and some of the money had not been returned. This, along with his salary check he had received the evening before, had all disappeared into the night.

"Two days later he phoned his sister instructing her to call his wife and inform her that he was not coming home again. Traffic tickets, revoked license, missing cash and a network of lies had created a life he could not face. He instructed her to make out as best she could and forget him as soon as possible. At that time no one knew where he was and it seemed all hope was gone for his return and reclamation.

"His wife called and I told her I would like to go over and talk to her. I realized that she needed Christ and the peace which only He can give. So I talked with her about the gospel after we had discussed Bryan's disappearance. Just then the words of Hebrews 1:14 came to my mind and I said to her, 'If we agree in prayer, God will answer by dispatching an angel to turn Bryan around right where he is and send him home.' In complete faith we knelt down in her living room and asked God to send an angel after her husband.

"I did not hear from her until she called my home at midnight. She was crying and said, 'I don't know what to say to you. My husband has just called! You have restored my faith and you have brought my husband home.'

" 'I had nothing to do with it,' I said, 'God has answered our prayers so you can get down on your knees and thank Him.'

"The next afternoon, her husband called me from the apartment asking me to come over. As I looked and listened, he related how he had been almost manhandled by God. It was as though an invincible physical force had grabbed him by the back of the neck and brought him home to the apartment! He found resistance was impossible!

"When I asked him if he would like to accept Jesus

as Lord of his life he cooperated with eagerness. And so, we knelt again in that living room as he invited the Lord Jesus Christ into his heart, and at the same time, to fill him with the Holy Spirit.

"I have never seen a person so dramatically changed. The facade that he had been wearing just dropped away. His looks, his very countenance changed. He became a new creation in Christ Jesus.

"Professionally he became one of my most responsible people and I eventually put him in charge of one of our very complicated multi-media projects. He became a dedicated family man too. God had rescued a man going under for the third time. I can never doubt that God sent one of His Holy Ones to place that man under arrest and return him under custody to his home and family and to God."

Yes, when the records are revealed we may discover that many people who responded to Billy Graham's invitations, or were led to Christ through personal witnessing, were strongly influenced in their decision by angels dispatched by the Holy Spirit. Accidents, near-tragedies, varieties of circumstances and great outpourings of God's goodness are consistently brought to pass by the Holy Ones in their involvement in evangelism.

Evangelism was born in the proclamation of an angel, "There has been born for you a Saviour, who is Christ the Lord." And the final evangelization of the world will be accomplished successfully by the Angel of Evangelism.

Today, wherever the gospel of the Lord Jesus Christ is proclaimed faithfully, we may be certain that in some way and to some extent the angels are involved, not only on earth, but also in resounding rejoicing in heaven over one sinner who repents. As the servants of Christ hold forth the Word and minister to those who sit in darkness and in the shadow of death, they themselves are being assisted in their work by the ministering spirits, "sent out to render service for the sake of those who will inherit salvation."[12]

Footnotes to Chapter 6
1. 2 Corinthians 5:18
2. Luke 2:10,11
3. Matthew 1:21
4. Matthew 28:6
5. Matthew 28:7
6. Acts 8:6,12
7. Acts 8:25,26
8. Acts 10:1-6
9. Acts 27:20
10. Acts 27:23-25
11. Revelation 14:6,7
12. Hebrews 1:14

CHAPTER 7

The Great, Great War

Would you be surprised if some morning you would find on the front page of your newspaper the screaming headlines: "WAR IN HEAVEN"?

The type has been set—in fact, the headlines have been already printed—in the Bible. "And THERE WAS WAR IN HEAVEN, Michael and his angels waging war with the dragon (Satan). And the dragon and his angels waged war, and they were not strong enough, and there was no longer a place found for them in heaven. And the great dragon was thrown down, the serpent of old who is called the Devil and Satan, who deceives the whole world; he was thrown down to the earth, and his angels were thrown down with him."[1]

Actually, the conflict as here described has not yet occurred. This is the prophetic view of one of the final battles in a war which has been raging for ages before the dawn of human history.

It all started when Lucifer, the wisest and most beautiful of all created beings, and probably the ruling prince of the angelic order, rebelled against the sovereignty of God. Isaiah's description of that act of treason is quite dramatic.

"How you have fallen from heaven, O star of the morning, son of the dawn! . . . You said in your heart, 'I will ascend to heaven; I will raise my throne above the stars of God, and I will sit on the mount of assembly in the recesses of the north. I will ascend above the heights of the clouds; I will make myself like the Most High.' "[2]

Using the king of Tyrus as an indirect means of addressing Satan, Ezekiel describes Lucifer before his rebellion, in glowing terms:

"You had the seal of perfection, full of wisdom and perfect in beauty. You were in Eden, the garden of God; every precious stone was your covering: the ruby, the topaz, and the diamond; the beryl, the onyx, and the jasper; the lapis lazuli, the turquoise, and the emerald; and the gold, the workmanship of your settings and sockets was in you. On the day that you were created they were prepared. You were the anointed cherub who covers (guards); and I placed you there. You were on the holy mountain of God; you walked in the midst of the stones of fire. You were blameless in your ways from the day you were created, until unrighteousness was found in you.

"By the abundance of your trade you were internally filled with violence, and you sinned; therefore I have cast you as profane from the mountain of God. And I have destroyed you, O covering (guardian) cherub, from the midst of the stones of fire.

"Your heart was lifted up because of your beauty; you corrupted your wisdom by reason of your splendor."[3]

And that's how it all started, and ever since the conflict has been raging between a holy God and an evil usurper. Naturally, the subjects of both kingdoms are involved in the hostilities.

There seems to be a possibility that when Lucifer rebelled against his Creator's sovereignty, one-third of the angelic hosts joined him in insurrection. In the Scriptures angels are sometimes referred to as "stars." In fact, Satan himself, prior to his fall was called the "star of the morning." In Revelation 12 where Satan is pictured as "a great red dragon," it is said that "his tail swept away a third of the stars of heaven, and threw them to the earth."[4]

Somewhere on or above this earth there is operating a vast and powerful kingdom of darkness. The apostle Paul wrote of Satan as "the prince of the power of the air . . . the spirit that is now working in the sons of disobedience."[5] Undoubtedly the Apostle was referring to the same prince of darkness and his legions of rebel angels, when he assured the Roman believers that not even "angels, nor principalities . . . shall be able to separate us from the love of God, which is in Christ Jesus our Lord."[6]

When writing to the Ephesian Christians, Paul warned them to "put on the full armor of God, that you may be able to stand firm against the schemes of the devil." He then referred to the organized kingdom of Satan as a dangerous and powerful force.

"For our struggle is not against flesh and blood, but against the rulers, against the powers, against the world-forces of this darkness, against the spiritual (superhuman) forces of wickedness in the heavenly places."

This superconflict between infernal and heavenly forces is operative in all areas of human experience. Satan and his demons are promoting the occult with all its ramifications, and the Holy Spirit and the Holy Ones are assisting in the extension of the worship and service of the Lord Jesus Christ. The drug culture, the racial, the generation, and all other gaps, the violent demonstrations, the wars and international tensions—all these are the products of the brain trust constantly operating in Satan's kingdom of darkness.

Few of us realize the extent of the involvement of the angelic forces in international politics and human events. Who would ever think that Satan would be interested in the burial of a human body? But he was, and it was an angel who opposed his attempt. Jude tells us: "Michael the archangel . . . disputed with the devil and argued about the body of Moses." We have no idea why the Devil desired that corpse, but want it he did. Perhaps he did not want God to have it to use many years later on the Mount of Transfiguration.

It is Daniel who most dramatically reveals the constant and bitter conflict between the Holy Ones and the angels of darkness in the realm of politics.

Daniel had vicariously confessed the sin of Israel and petitioned God for the restoration of the nation. He then fasted for three weeks. The very day that Daniel prayed and began his fast, one of the Holy Ones was given God's reply to Daniel's prayer, and was sent from heaven to earth to deliver the communication to the prophet. BUT IT TOOK HIM THREE WEEKS TO ARRIVE! Let's listen in as he tells Daniel why it took so long.

"O Daniel, man of high esteem, understand the words that I am about to tell you and stand upright, for I have now been sent to you. . . . Do not be afraid, Daniel, for from the first day that you set your heart on understanding this and on humbling yourself before your God, your words were heard, and I have come in response to your words. But the prince of the kingdom of Persia was withstanding me for twenty-one days; then behold, Michael, one of the chief princes, came to help me, for I had been left there with the kings of Persia. Now I have come to give you an understanding of what will happen to your people in the latter days."[9]

Satan had stationed one of his most powerful demons at the capital of the Persian kingdom. And so powerful was that demon that he was able to arrest the progress of the Holy One until Michael, the archangel, came to assist him! The narration of the Holy One continues.

"I shall now return to fight against the prince (Satanic angel) of Persia; so I am going forth, and behold, the prince of Greece is about to come. . . . (Yet there is no one who stands firmly with me against these forces except Michael your prince. And in the first year of Darius the Mede I arose to be an encouragement and a protection for him.)"[10]

This amazing information is tremendously significant!

Demons, powerful enough to interfere with the ministry of God's angels are apparently located at every important political center. They do all they can to prevent the will of God being done on earth as it is in heaven. On the other hand, God's Holy Ones are dedicated to the fulfillment of God's will. Frequently these cross-purposes lead to violent conflict between the demons and God's angels who sometimes are forced to call for reinforcements.

There are times when the Holy Ones take the offensive against the powers of darkness ("I shall now return to fight against the prince of Persia"), and the attacked demon is then compelled to call for assistance ("the prince of Greece is about to come").

It is important to realize that this political involvement of the angelic order is not one-sided. The Holy Ones also exert a powerful influence in the political arena. The angel who came to Daniel informed the prophet that "in the first year of (the reign of) Darius the Mede I arose to be an encouragement and a protection for" the king. And Darius proved himself a mighty king indeed.

When we no longer see through a glass darkly, but face to face, and know as we are known, probably we will be astonished to discover the tremendous influence the Holy Ones had in the national elections of our presidents and the acquisition of power by the leaders of other nations. The real struggles for power do not take place at the national conventions of the various political powers, but in the realms of principalities and powers where demons and the Holy Ones continue their conflict of the ages.

Satan may seem to win some important battles, but the outcome of the war is certain. Michael and the Holy Ones will finally shatter the powers of dark-

ness and cast Satan and his rebel angels out of heaven.
And we shall share in that victory! John tells us of
our involvement in that thrilling conquest:

"I heard a loud voice in heaven, saying, 'Now the
salvation, and the power, and the kingdom of our
God and the authority of His Christ have come, for
the accuser of our brethren has been thrown down,
who accuses them before our God day and night.
And they overcame him because of the blood of the
Lamb and because of the word of their testimony."[11]

"Thanks be to God, who gives us the victory
through our Lord Jesus Christ."[12]

Footnotes to Chapter 7
1. Revelation 12:7-9
2. Isaiah 14:12-14
3. Ezekiel 28:12-17
4. Revelation 12:3,4
5. Ephesians 2:2
6. Romans 8:38,39
7. Ephesians 6:11,12
8. Jude 9
9. Daniel 10:11-14
10. Daniel 10:20,21; 11:1
11. Revelation 12:10,11
12. 1 Corinthians 15:57

CHAPTER 8

Energizers

Angels involved in physical therapy? Seems rather preposterous, doesn't it? But involved they have been and probably are today. The Bible does not contain a great deal of information concerning this activity of the Holy Ones. However, there are several instances where angels were sent to minister to the physical needs of God's servants.

In a previous chapter we saw how one of the Holy Ones came to the prophet Elijah when he was physically and emotionally at the end of the road. Two hot meals and refreshing water provided by the angel enabled the prophet to journey without additional nourishment for forty days and nights.

During the earthly ministry of the Lord Jesus Christ, upon two occasions He was the recipient of physical assistance from the Holy Ones.

Following His baptism by John in the Jordan River, Jesus was impelled by the Holy Spirit to go into the wilderness. There He was tempted by Satan for forty days. The searing heat of the wilderness, the increasing hunger and exhausting strain of the conflict of the ages took their toll of the physical strength of Christ. When finally Satan was routed and left the battlefield in defeat, "angels came and began to minister to Him."[1] It was this infusion of physical energy which enabled our Lord to return "to Galilee in the power of the Spirit. . . . and He began teaching in their synagogues."[2]

Christ's second experience with the Holy Ones came near the end of His pre-crucifixion ministry. He had met with His disciples for the Passover feast and had instituted the sacrament of Communion. After singing a hymn, they left the upper room and wended their way to the garden of Gethsemane. Upon arriving there, "Jesus . . . said to His disciples, 'Sit here while I go over there and pray.' And He took with Him Peter and the two sons of Zebedee, and began to be grieved and distressed.

"Then He said to them, 'My soul is deeply grieved, to the point of death; remain here and keep watch with Me.' And He went a little beyond them, and fell on His face and prayed, saying, 'My Father, if it is possible, let this cup pass from Me; yet not as I will, but as Thou wilt.'"[3]

As Jesus continued to bear our griefs and carry our sorrows, the crushing load became more than even Christ could bear. "And being in agony He was praying very fervently; and His sweat became like drops of blood, falling down upon the ground. . . . Now an angel from heaven appeared to Him, strengthening Him."[4]

This experience of Jesus' probably has been repeated many thousands of times in the lives of God's servants. When they reach the end of endurance, when strength has failed, and it is impossible to preach another sermon or teach another lesson, when nerves are strained to the breaking point—then there comes a sudden infusion of vitality and strength, a new lease on life. Who can say that their emotional and physical revival was not the result of divine therapy administered by one of the Holy Ones?

A pastor who has enjoyed more than usual success and blessing in his ministry said, "There have been many occasions when I have stood before my congregations to proclaim the Word of God, that I was so weak and ill I thought that at any moment I might faint. I had to hold on to the pulpit for support. And then something wonderful, something beautiful, happened. Suddenly there came over me a strange and delightful feeling of warmth and strength. My weakness and weariness vanished and I was filled with a sense of power and a vitality more than physical! And the wonder of it was, this strange sense of well-being continued with me long after my preaching and the service had concluded."

In his Gospel, the apostle John cites another case of physical assistance by the Holy Ones. Although some authorities question the authenticity of the statement in question, many other authorities insert, wholly or in part, between verses three and five of the fifth chapter of John, "waiting for the moving of the waters; for an angel of the Lord went down at certain seasons into the pool, and stirred up the water; whoever then first after the stirring up of the water stepped in was made well from whatever disease with which he was afflicted."[5]

While it is not our purpose to enter into this disagreement of biblical scholars, it is fitting that we point out that without the insertion of this statement, the sixth verse of the chapter makes no sense whatever. When the lame man was asked by Jesus if he wished to get well, he replied, "Sir, I have no man to put me into the pool when the water is stirred up, but while I am coming, another steps down before me."[6] We are therefore suggesting that through a method we do not understand, God was pleased in His grace and mercy to periodically send one of His Holy Ones to bring physical renewal through the "stirred up" waters of the pool of Bethesda.

Before leaving this subject, there is one more case we should examine. "In the third year of Cyrus, king of Persia a message was revealed to Daniel." The prophet wrote, "In those days I, Daniel, had been mourning for three entire weeks. I did not eat any tasty food, nor did meat or wine enter my mouth, nor did I use ointment at all, until the entire three weeks were completed."

Then there came to Daniel a "great vision; yet no strength was left in me, for my natural color turned to a deathly pallor, and I retained no strength. . . . And behold, one who resembled a human being was touching my lips; then I opened my mouth and spoke, and said to him who was standing before me, 'O my Lord, as a result of the vision anguish has come upon me, and I have retained no strength.' . . . Then this one with human appearance touched me again and strengthened me."[7]

Weakened by prolonged fasting and then drained of all remaining strength by the fright of the great vision, it was the reviving touch of the Holy One that brought Daniel to his feet and enabled him to receive and understand the divine prophetic message.

Mr. Homer Gail Crisman spent seventy years as a missionary in South America, working under the Christian and Missionary Alliance. Those early days of missionary life were days of persecution, uncertainty, almost constant traveling, either on foot or by horseback, and the responsibilities were heavy.

Mr. Crisman never was robust and many times despaired of life, but he had a strong faith in God as his keeper and physician.

One time in Colombia, too weak to claim deliverance for himself, he asked the Lord to lay him upon someone's heart. A man in Santa Ana, California, was awakened from a sound sleep, rather violently *shaken as if by an unseen hand,* and told to get up and pray for Mr. Crisman. This he did, and God's healing power was manifested *at the same time,* thousands of miles away, in the body of His servant!

Who did the shaking and gave the command to pray? Without doubt, it was one of the Holy Ones.

In the weakest moment of your life, when physically and emotionally you are totally exhausted, when collapse seems imminent, don't be surprised if suddenly, and for no apparent reason, your weakness is replaced by strength and your weariness by a delightful sense of well-being. God has sent one of His Holy Ones to touch you and thus fulfill His promise:

"He gives strength to the weary, and to him who

lacks might He increases power. Though youths grow weary and tired, and vigorous young men stumble badly, yet those who wait for the Lord will gain new strength; they will mount up with wings like eagles, they will run and not get tired, they will walk and not become weary."[8]

Footnotes to Chapter 8

1. Matthew 4:11
2. Luke 4:14,15
3. Matthew 26:36-39
4. Luke 22:44,43
5. John 5:4 (marginal note)
6. John 5:7
7. Daniel 10:1-3,8,16,18
8. Isaiah 40:29-31

CHAPTER 9

The Protectors

Saints of all ages have found strength and courage in moments of fearful danger in David's familiar words, "The angel of the Lord encamps around those who fear Him and rescues them."[1]

The angel of the Lord delivered Daniel from the fangs and claws of the lions. The Holy Ones delivered the three Hebrew children from the deadly flames of Nebuchadnezzar's burning fiery furnace. A Holy One delivered Isaac from the sacrificial knife of his father, Abraham. An angel delivered Peter from Herod's prison and sword. And God's Holy Ones are actively engaged here and now in delivering and protecting God's children.

In his book, *Providential Deliverances,* W. A. Spicer tells of an experience a Christian colporteur had in Norway. In attempting to reach families living in a hidden valley, he had to descend a dangerous mountain trail. At one steep, dangerous place he stopped to pray, asking God to send His angel to go with him. He safely reached the valley.

At the first cottage he met a man and his wife, who, it seems, had been watching his descent of the dangerous trail.

"What has become of your companion?" was their first question after the usual greeting.

"What companion?" asked the missionary.

"The man who was with you."

"But there was no one with me; I am traveling alone."

"Is that possible?" they exclaimed in surprise. "We were watching you as you came down the mountain, and it really seemed to us that there were two men crossing the mountain together."

"Then," reported missionary Hokland, "I was reminded of my prayer to God for help, and of the word of the Lord in Psalm 34:7, 'The angel of the Lord encampeth round about them that fear him and delivereth them.' "

In 1924, Mr. Crisman, referred to in a previous chapter, along with his wife, went to Ipiales, Colombia. Many country districts were visited and the work seemed encouraging, with sometimes as many as 120 in attendance at the meetings.

The opposition became strong and throughout 1926 they noted an unaccustomed fear and coldness on the part of the people.

Following a Wednesday night meeting, just as the congregation was leaving, a shower of stones came at the front door and all had to remain inside until 11:30 before they could venture out.

The following night there was a prayer meeting, and again the mob started to throw stones as the meeting was dismissed. They began to batter the door with a heavy log and it started to yield. There were five men inside the building but what could five men do against a multitude? When they saw the door was being broken open, everyone retreated to the second floor.

The door went down and the frenzied mob rushed inside and, yelling at the top of their voices, they began breaking doors and windows and furniture. It appeared that the end had come for the little body of believers.

The mob arrived at the foot of the stairs and stopped there! It seemed as if an unseen hand had stayed them and not a man was able to move up those stairs! For two hours they attempted to get to the believers and then, crestfallen, they left the building. Later sixty-five stones were picked up from that room—stones the Holy Ones would not permit to be thrown at God's threatened children.

Several years ago, while touring the Holy Land, our group arrived at the ancient city of Ephesus. In attempting to get a good photograph of those remarkable ruins, the slab of marble I was standing on tilted, and I fell backwards into an excavation about ten-feet deep, the bottom of which was littered with jagged fragments of marble. As I began to fall, there was, for a flashing moment, a sense of terrible fear; and then instantly *the fear and feel of falling vanished* and I seemed to be floating, rather than falling down. It was as though strong hands were under me, gently lowering me to the bottom of the excavation. Apart from my arm hitting my glasses against my eyebrow, causing a slight laceration, I had no other injury. To the amazement of the other members of our tour group, after being helped out of the excavation, I was able to continue the tour without pain or discomfort.

While I realize that the ninety-first Psalm has Messianic application, I cannot help feeling that what happened to me at Ephesus was a definite fulfillment of God's wonderful promise, "For He will give His angels charge concerning you; to guard you in all your ways. They will bear you up in their hands, lest you strike your foot against a stone"![2] And certainly, not one member of our tour party would ever deny that the Holy Ones were involved in this miraculous deliverance.

Mr. Homer Gifford of Wycliffe Bible Translators tells the following story of angelic activity in Mexico:

"Several years ago a missionary, named Egbert Dyck, went to a Tzeltal settlement to witness to some of the Indians. He stayed two weeks, then kept going back. All but one man in the village became Christians—about one hundred families. There was much persecution and eventually the entire village moved to the present site of Santo Domingo and established a Christian community.

"Near the Christian village there was a pagan village in which lived a very wicked and possibly demon-possessed man named Domingo Hermandez who bitterly hated the Christians. He was determined to burn their village and to slaughter all its inhabitants. He organized his fellow villagers and prepared firebrands and canoes. Late one night he led his men down the hill, across the river and approached the Christian village. Suddenly they saw a bright light shining through the windows of every home in the village! Then a strange glare of light broke over the entire village!

"Domingo Hermandez and his men were so frightened that they turned and ran down the hill, plunged into the river, swam across and ran, soaking wet, the half mile to their village.

"Next morning as the women from the pagan village were washing their clothes in the river, they called across to the Christian women on the other side of the river, 'What were those strange lights in your huts last night?'

"The Christian women replied, 'What lights? We had no lights burning. We were sound asleep.' "

True, they had no lights burning, but the Holy Ones did! They brought a little of that glory of the Lord that shone on the hills of Bethlehem more than nineteen hundred years ago and let it shine in those Christian huts and over that Christian village.

Another thrilling story of angelic intervention begins with Ken Weathers, also of Wycliffe Bible Translators, conducting a school among the Chenalho people of Mexico. A young Mintontic student named Erasto attended the school, accepted Christ and then led a fellow Mintontic named Vincente to a saving knowledge of our Lord.

Vincente was greatly used of God and, as the power of the Holy Spirit was manifested, many pagans were led to repentance and faith in Christ. Then the Power of Darkness began to marshal his forces to counterattack. Persecution grew until the lives of the Mintontic Christians were in constant danger. Finally the men hid their wives and children in a cave for their protection. But the enemies of the church were aware of the believers' hiding place and one night they decided to attack and kill everyone they found there.

The version of what happened at the cave depends upon whether the story is told by the Christians or by their enemies.

The enemies testify that as they approached the cave, when they came within a few yards of the entrance, they were held back in terror by ferocious dogs guarding the opening!

The believers say that they saw the armed men approaching boldly, but as they came within a few yards of the cave they suddenly stopped, looking quite terrified, then turned and, screaming with fear, they fled from the cave. But the believers neither saw nor did they hear any dogs.

Upon an earlier occasion some men had planned to go to Vincente's house and kill him. But as they neared his house they found it surrounded by a veritable army of mounted soldiers! The would-be murderers and the nearby townfolk were thrown into a panic thinking that they were about to be attacked by Vincente's protectors.

"Incredible! Impossible!" you may say. Not at all. These things have really happened and they are still happening around the world. Thousands of people may be worshiping Satan and demon activity may be increasing at an alarming rate. The Devil may be alive, and through his agents, may be very active on this earth. But he also is having his problems—*with the Holy Ones.* They are very real, also very much alive, and very active ministering to those who have needs, protecting those who are in danger, and delivering the heirs of salvation to whom they minister.

Footnotes to Chapter 9
1. Psalm 34:7
2. Psalm 91:11,12

CHAPTER 10

Angels in Prophecy

What does the future hold for this weary old world? for the nation of Israel? for the physical earth? The answers to such questions are not to be found in astrology or necromancy but in the divinely inspired Word of God. And we may be certain that, as the passing of time fulfills the prophetic Scriptures, the Holy Ones will be deeply involved in that fulfillment.

This is illustrated by the prophet Daniel as he presents a graphic description of "the man of lawlessness . . . the son of destruction," and called by John "the beast,"[1] who will appear on earth and establish his kingdom during the Great Tribulation:

"The king will do as he pleases, and he will exalt and magnify himself above every god, and will speak monstrous things against the God of gods. . . . He will also enter the Beautiful Land, and many countries will fall; . . . And he will pitch the tents of his royal pavilion between the seas and the beautiful Holy Mountain; yet he will come to his end, and no one will help him."[2]

Then the prophet continues, "Now at that time Michael, the great prince who stands guard over the sons of your people, will arise. And there will be a time of distress such as has never occurred since there was a nation until that time; and at that time your people, everyone who is found written in the book, will be rescued."[3]

Here the Bible introduces to us the aggressive part that angels will play in the fulfillment of prophetic Scriptures. When the nation of Israel will pass through the darkest hour of its history, and all hope for survival fades, heaven then will spring into action and Michael, that great angelic guardian of Israel, will arise to defend those "written in the book."

In the Gospels we find twenty-two verses where Jesus referred to the Holy Ones. Fourteen of these references have to do with the participation of angels in the fulfillment of prophecy. These deserve our attention.

Matthew informs us that one day "Jesus went out of the house, and was sitting by the sea. And great multitudes gathered about Him, so that He got into a boat and sat down, and the whole multitude was standing on the beach. And He spoke many things to them in parables."[4]

Among the parables taught that day was the one about the wheat and the tares. After Jesus "left the multitudes, and went into the house. . . . His disciples came to Him, saying, 'Explain to us the parable of the tares of the field.'

"And He answered and said, 'The one who sows the good seed is the Son of Man, and the field is the world; and as for the good seed, these are the sons of the kingdom; and the tares are the sons of the evil one; and the enemy who sowed them is the devil, and the harvest is the end of the age; and the reapers are angels. Therefore, just as the tares are gathered up and burned with fire, so shall it be at the end of the age.

" 'The Son of Man will send forth His angels, and they will gather out of His kingdom all stumbling blocks, and those who commit lawlessness, and will cast them into the furnace of fire; in that place there shall be weeping and gnashing of teeth.'

" 'Then the righteous will shine forth as the sun in the kingdom of their Father.' "[5]

Jesus reiterated this same responsibility of the Holy Ones in verse 49 of the same chapter. "So it will be at the end of the age; the angels shall come forth, and take the wicked from among the righteous."

Both these prophecies of Jesus reveal to us that angels will be used as instruments of judgment at the revelation of Christ. In a previous chapter, we saw that the Holy Ones have the blessed and comforting responsibility of carrying the righteous dead into the presence of God. Here we see the other side of the coin. The wicked, condemned by God to eternal judgment, will be conveyed to their place of torment by the same creatures of light, the Holy Ones.

Prophecy not only pictures the angels as messengers

of judgments, but also as sharing in the glory of the second advent of the Lord Jesus Christ. When our Lord comes to establish His millennial kingdom—lifting the curse of sin; restoring the Edenic bliss and beauty; causing the wolf to dwell with the lamb—then the myriads of angels shall come with Him in visible glory.

This is how Jesus Himself described this future event: "When the Son of Man comes in His glory, and all the angels with Him, then He will sit on His glorious throne. . . . And He will send forth His angels with a great trumpet and they will gather together His elect from the four winds, from one end of the sky to the other."[6] Of that same coming day, the apostle Paul wrote that "The Lord Jesus shall be revealed from heaven with His mighty angels in flaming fire."[7]

Christ also referred to a time when He would present His beloved followers to the Holy Ones. We cannot be certain of the time or the circumstances when this will occur, but apparently He was anticipating the moment when it would be His pleasure to introduce His beloved ones individually to the Holy Ones. Jesus said, "Everyone who confesses Me before men, the Son of Man shall confess him also before the angels of God."[8]

Tragically, some who profess to follow and serve Christ will not be found worthy of this honor, for Jesus continued, "But he who denies Me before men shall be denied before the angels of God."[9]

There can be no doubt that we are approaching or have already entered the end times. The coming of the Lord for His bride is drawing nigh. The "blessed hope" of the Church is about to be realized.

Wars, international tensions, earthquakes, famines, pestilences, social gaps, moral degeneration with its homosexuality, pornography and amorality, ecological pollutions, inflation, occultism, spiritual decline—these all are part of the same weather map—the storm of judgment is about to break upon the world in all its fury.

Dark days, indeed, and yet it is the glorious dawn of the best day of all for the children of God! Why? Because Jesus is coming! Paul tells us about it. And in doing so, he informs us that in this event, also, the Holy Ones will be involved.

"The Lord Himself will descend from heaven with a shout, with the voice of the archangel, and with the trumpet of God; and the dead in Christ shall rise first.

"Then we who are alive and remain shall be caught up together with them in the clouds to meet the Lord in the air, and thus we shall always be with the Lord."[10]

That phrase, "the voice of the archangel," is both interesting and mysterious. What part will Michael, the great archangel, play in the rapture of the Church? What will he say when the Lord descends from heaven with a shout? Why will he be involved in the Second Appearing of Christ? These questions cannot be answered now. God draws the curtain of secrecy and says, "Not now, but later you will know as you are known."

Going now from the Gospels and the epistles of the New Testament, we turn our attention to its only prophetic book. Here we find a multiplicity of angelic involvements, most of them in the application of judgment.

Undoubtedly, when Jesus addressed His messages to the "angels" of the Asiatic churches, He had in mind the human "messengers" or leaders of those churches. But apart from these instances there is to be found in this book more than fifty references to the Holy Ones!

The book of Revelation consists largely of prophecies dealing with future judgments. In biblical history we find that angels have been used frequently as messengers of judgment. It is therefore not surprising to find them described repeatedly in Revelation as operating in the same role.

It came as quite a surprise to the apostle John! While exiled on the island of Patmos he was engaged in worship one Lord's day when he heard behind him a loud voice commissioning him to write letters from Jesus Christ to seven of the churches in Asia. John completed the assignment, and then came the big surprise. From the azure dome of the skies the same loud voice was heard, but this time in invitation, "Come up here, and I will show you what must take place after these things."[11]

To John's amazement, the next moment he found himself standing in the presence of the Lord God Almighty! Clasped in the right hand of God was a seven-sealed book. It was then John began to realize that from this point on, he would be led into amazing revelations of God's plan and program by the Holy Ones. And it was an angel who proclaimed with a loud voice, "Who is worthy to open the book and to break its seals"?[12]

Upon the discovery of the Lamb as the only one worthy of this task, John heard the voice of many angels who were standing around the throne of God—"myriads of myriads, and thousands of thousands; saying with a loud voice, 'Worthy is the Lamb that was slain to receive power and riches and wisdom and might and honor and glory and blessing.' "[13]

Then John saw four angels standing at the four corners of the earth, holding back the four winds of the earth. Another angel was seen coming from the east, ordering the four angels of the winds not to harm the earth until God's servants were sealed for their protection.[14]

In chapter 8 of this prophetic book John tells about more of the Holy Ones: the seven angels who will usher in upon the defiant kingdom of the Beast the disastrous trumpet judgments; the priest-angel who will offer upon the golden altar of heaven the holy incense and the prayers of the saints.

As the revealing of God's program of judgment continues, we join with John in beholding a veritable parade of the Holy Ones. In chapter 9 there is the angel of the bottomless pit, or the abyss, who loosens the plague of torturing locusts upon the inhabitants of earth; and the four angels "prepared for the hour and day and month and year . . . so that they might kill a third of mankind" with their monster horsemen numbering two hundred million!

In chapter 10 we are shown the "rainbow angel" who tells John to eat the little book of judgment he held in his hand. When John obeyed, he found it was a sweet little morsel to taste, but suffered stomach cramps in consequence.

Chapter 12 gives to us that terse little account of the greatest battle of all eternity! In comparison, Armageddon will be child's play, for this will be a battle of supercreatures from out in space—space beyond the furthest galaxy—in the limitless expanses of heaven itself!

Tension had been building up for innumerable millenniums. Ever since the original insurrection under the leadership of Lucifer, a final conflict was inevitable. That tragic incident in the Garden of Eden sealed the death warrant of Lucifer and it was only a matter of time until the "Seed of the woman" would fatally bruise his head.

Of course, the Prince of Darkness did everything in his power to avoid his fate. The progressive moral and spiritual degeneration of the nation through which was to come the promised Seed—David's immoral involvement with Bathsheba, the destruction of Israel and Judah as national entities, Herod's attempt to murder the Child of Bethlehem, the efforts of the Jewish elders to destroy the Nazarene—all these were futile attempts by Satan to prevent the fatal stroke he would receive through Christ's accomplishments at the cross and at the sepulcher.

Although fatally wounded at Calvary, Satan has continued to attempt by every possible means to avoid his final defeat and doom. He used Saul of Tarsus; Nero and the Roman persecutions, both political and ecclesiastic; the Spanish Inquisition; apostate German theologians, liberal theology and dialectic materialism. So Satan's efforts continue into our day.

Through the drug and occult cultures; through neoorthodoxy; through communism and through godless education; through the temperature drop in Christian love and the substitution of a form of godliness for the power it should manifest; through the adoption of program rather than Spirit in worship; through divisions in the body of Christ—all these are convulsive efforts by the powers of darkness to survive. But there is no possibility of their succeeding in spite of clever designs and powerful resources.

The battle lines are being drawn! At last it will be impossible for any further delay in the final conflict. With his prophetic vision, John saw it happen. "THERE WAS WAR IN HEAVEN!"

Michael, the mighty archangel, assembles his angelic forces and declares war against the disenfranchised Lucifer! Simultaneously the Prince of Darkness declares a state of war against the Holy Ones! What human mind could even imagine the fury and the forces involved in such a conflict?

Never for one moment was there any doubt as to who would be the victor. Even though they threw all their infernal energies into the conflict, Satan and his angels "were not strong enough, and there was no longer a place found for them in heaven. And the great dragon was thrown down, the serpent of old who is called the Devil and Satan, who deceives the whole world; he was thrown down to the earth, and his angels were thrown down with him."[15]

During the dark days of the Great Tribulation, when it will seem that all light has gone out—the church has been caught up to be with Christ, the personal presence of the Holy Spirit has been withdrawn, and there will be a famine for the Word of God—then will appear, flying in midheaven, "another

97

angel." This is the angel of evangelism, "having an eternal gospel to preach to those who live on the earth, and to every nation and tribe and tongue and people."[16]

He is followed in the prophetic revelation by five more angels, each having specific responsibilities. The first pronounces woe upon that wicked metropolis of sin, Babylon of the future. The second Holy One warns the worshipers of the Beast that they will be forced to drink of the wine of the wrath of God in eternal torment.

The third angel calls for the Son of Man to put in His sickle and reap the ripe harvest of the earth. The fourth angel is seen coming out of the temple in heaven with another sharp sickle.

The fifth angel in chapter 14 of Revelation is described as, "another angel, the one who has power over fire." He called with a loud voice "to him who had the sharp sickle, saying, 'Put in your sharp sickle, and gather the clusters from the vine of the earth, because her grapes are ripe.' And the angel swung his sickle to the earth, and gathered the clusters from the vine of the earth, and threw them into the great wine press of the wrath of God."[17]

This interesting passage throws light on the mechanics of Armageddon. While it will be the Lord Jesus Christ who will tread the wine press of Armageddon, it will be the duty of the Holy Ones to gather the armies of the world and assemble them in the plains of Megiddo, the valley of Jehoshaphat, where the wine press will be "trodden outside the city, and blood (will come) out from the wine press, up to the horses' bridles, for a distance of two hundred miles."[18]

As we continue to follow the involvement of the Holy Ones in this prophetic Scripture, we find in chapter 15 seven angels "who had seven plagues, which are the last, because in them the wrath of God is finished." They come out of the temple of the tabernacle of testimony in heaven, and they are clothed in linen, clean and bright, and girded around their breasts with golden girdles.

As their bowls of judgment are poured out upon a God-hating, Beast-worshiping world, these seven angels will bring unprecedented horror upon an already stricken earth. Loathsome and malignant sores, seas and sources of drinking water turned into blood, scorching heat from an overheated sun, a darkness so painful that men will gnaw their tongues in agony, deadly lightnings, an earthquake of unprecedented magnitude that destroys the cities of the world, and huge hailstones, each about one hundred pounds. These will comprise the harvest of wrath brought to the men of earth by God's Holy Ones.

The final chapter in the history of the world's capital of iniquity, believed by many Bible students to be Rome, is revealed in Revelation 17 and 18. John is given a tour and shown an exposure of the vile metropolis of sin by one of the seven angels of the bowl judgments. Then he is granted a preview of the final and complete destruction of that city by "another angel coming down from heaven, having great authority, and the earth was illuminated with his glory."[19] At the end of this preview of judgment, John saw "a strong angel" who took up a stone like a great millstone and threw it into the sea, saying, "Thus will Babylon, the great city, be thrown down with violence, and will not be found any longer."[20]

In chapter 19 of the prophecy we have a dramatic and thrilling picture of the revelation of the Lord Jesus Christ in flaming fire executing judgments upon the Beast and his armies. Here again we see angelic involvement. John wrote, "I saw an angel standing in the sun; and he cried out with a loud voice, saying to all the birds which fly in midheaven, 'Come, assemble for the great supper of God; in order that you may eat the flesh of kings and the flesh of commanders and the flesh of mighty men and the flesh of horses and of those who sit on them and the flesh of all men, both free men and slaves, and small and great.' "[21]

The final judgment activity of the Holy Ones shown to us in prophetic Scripture is found in chapter 20 of Revelation: "And I saw an angel coming down from heaven, having the key of the abyss and a great chain in his hand. And he laid hold of the dragon, the serpent of old, who is the Devil and Satan, and bound him for a thousand years, and threw him into the abyss, and shut it and sealed it over him, so that he should not deceive the nations any longer, until the thousand years were completed."[22]

One of the seven angels who had poured his bowl of plagues upon the earth had a dual responsibility. It was a pleasant one, a responsibility that brought tremendous delight and joy to the heart of John. The Holy One said, "Come here, I shall show you the bride, the wife of the Lamb."[23] And then he took the apostle on a tour of the bride's home, the place

Jesus had in mind when He said to His disciples, "I go to prepare a place for you."

For John's benefit, the angel guide measured the city and described the building material used in its construction. Then they went into the city and the Holy One pointed out the river of life, coming from the throne of God and of the Lamb; the tree of life growing on both sides of the river; the illumination of the city by the Lord God Himself; and the total absence of anything that would defile the city or its inhabitants.

John was so overwhelmed by the wonder and glory of it all that he fell down to worship at the feet of the angel who showed him these things. Then the Holy One said something very significant:

"Do not do that; I am a fellow-servant of yours and of your brethren the prophets and of those who heed the words of this book: worship God."[24]

In making this statement the angel emphasized his status in God's organization. Although belonging to a higher order than man, he, like man, was only a servant of God; and included in that classification of servants are not only the apostles and prophets, but also all *those who heed the words* of this divine revelation of Jesus Christ.

There is only one more reference to the Holy Ones in this book and it comes from the lips of the Lamb:

"I, Jesus, have sent My angel to testify to you these things for the churches. I am the root and the off-spring of David, the bright morning star."[25]

Yes, angels of all degrees of glory, power, authority and purpose are to be found in prophetic Scripture. They will bring comfort and assurance to God's own, and suffering and anguish to those who receive not the love of the truth that they might be saved.

Footnotes to Chapter 10
1. 2 Thessalonians 2:3; Revelation 11:7
2. Daniel 11:36-45
3. Daniel 12:1
4. Matthew 13:1-3
5. Matthew 13:36-43
6. Matthew 25:31; 24:31
7. 2 Thessalonians 1:7
8. Luke 12:8
9. Luke 12:9
10. 1 Thessalonians 4:16,17
11. Revelation 4:1
12. Revelation 5:2
13. Revelation 5:11,12
14. Revelation 7:1-3
15. Revelation 12:7,8
16. Revelation 14:6
17. Revelation 14:18,19
18. Revelation 14:20
19. Revelation 18:1
20. Revelation 18:21
21. Revelation 19:17,18
22. Revelation 20:1-3
23. Revelation 21:9
24. Revelation 22:9
25. Revelation 22:16

CHAPTER 11

The Avengers

The activity of angels as ministers of judgment has not been limited to the *prophetic* Scriptures. At various times they have been used of God in drastic punitive action, especially upon those nations hostile to Israel.

Traditionally we think of angels as beautiful, protective guardians of a child crossing a narrow, dangerous bridge. Or we may picture them as lovely, winged creatures with golden trumpets, welcoming the saints into a radiant paradise. True, there have been many times when their appearance occasioned great joy and heralded a miraculous deliverance for the people of God. But there have been other times when their coming brought terror and death. To God's people they usually minister assistance and blessing. To the enemies of God, they sometimes minister death, acting as "a band of destroying angels."[1]

In a previous chapter we saw the good King Hezekiah take the threatening letter he had received from the general of the Assyrian army into the house of God and spread it open before the Lord. The Lord God read the letter and then sent His prophet Isaiah to give the Lord's reaction to Hezekiah.

Isaiah reported back to the king: "Therefore thus says the Lord concerning the king of Assyria, 'He shall not come to this city or shoot an arrow there; neither shall he come before it with a shield, nor throw up a mound against it. By the way that he came, by the same shall he return, and he shall not come to this city,' declares the Lord. 'For I will defend this city to save it for My own sake and for My servant David's sake.'

"Then it happened that night that the angel of the Lord went out, and struck 185,000 in the camp of the Assyrians; and when men rose early in the morning, behold, all of them were dead bodies.

"So Sennacherib king of Assyria departed and returned home, and lived in Nineveh. And it came about as he was worshiping in the house of Nisroch his god, that Adrammelech and Sharezer killed him with the sword."[2]

When David, motivated by pride, took a forbidden census of the men of Israel, the avengers were sent from heaven to punish this act of disobedience. "Seventy thousand men of the people from Dan to Beersheba died. When the angel stretched out his hand toward Jerusalem to destroy it, the Lord relented from the calamity, and said to the angel who destroyed the people, 'It is enough! Now relax your hand!' "[3]

In New Testament history we find another case

where the avengers struck an arrogant enemy of the Lord.

Earlier we mentioned that King Herod had executed James and then arrested Peter, intending to murder him after the Passover feast. But in answer to prayer Peter was delivered by an angel from the hand of Herod. But God was not yet finished with Herod.

The citizens of Tyre and Sidon came to Herod to crave his cooperation in a trade pact. "On an appointed day Herod, having put on his royal apparel, took his seat on the rostrum and began delivering an address to them. And the people kept crying out, 'The voice of a god and not of a man!' And immediately an angel of the Lord struck him because he did not give God the glory, and he was eaten by worms and died. But the word of the Lord continued to grow and to be multiplied."[4]

God will not always tolerate blasphemy and open opposition to His will and plan. The writer of the book of Hebrews warns us, "It is a terrifying thing to fall into the hands of the living God."[5]

Several years ago a troop of young Jeunesse rebels came into a Congo village. The leader asked of one of the villagers, "What is that house?"

"That is the house of God," was the reply.

The leader of the rebels picked up a stone to throw into it. At that instant he was killed by a bullet accidently fired by one of his own men!

In another village the rebels met in a hut to plan the slaughter of all the Christians in the immediate area. In the meanwhile a storm arose. There was a blinding flash as lightning struck that very hut. Every rebel was instantly killed! In both cases the Holy Ones, acting as God's avengers, had administered divine judgment.

In southeastern Pennsylvania there is a little farming village named Vera Cruz. Many years ago a prosperous farmer, Mr. Musselman, lived there and established a little Bible teaching ministry which later developed into the Mennonite Brethren in Christ denomination. He was a very godly man and noted throughout the community for his generosity and holy life. One clear cold winter night he and his wife awakened to find a man standing by their bed, with a sharp ax raised over his head. With foul language he threatened to steal all their valuables and chop them to pieces. At that moment the old farmer became conscious of the peace that passeth all understanding and, looking up into the passion-twisted face of the intruder, he said, "My dear friend, my God will not permit you to harm us, His angel is here to protect us."

At that instant the man's arms became paralyzed and the heavy ax clattered to the floor. His arms fell helplessly to his sides!

The Musselmans arose and led the terrified man downstairs and seated him at the kitchen table. Mother Musselman prepared him some food and the old farmer spoon-fed him. They told him about the love of God, prayed for him, and then led him to the door and he disappeared into the night.

One of the avengers had struck again and another wicked creature had discovered that it really is a terrifying thing to fall into the hands of the living God.

There is so much that we do not know. Eternity will probably reveal that many incidents called "accidents" by the news media, were actually visitations of judgment by the Holy Ones—God's avengers.

The Lord God's antediluvian warning has never been withdrawn. He said then, and He says today:

"My Spirit shall not strive with man forever."[6]

"Today if you hear His voice, do not harden your hearts."[7]

"Seek the Lord while He may be found; call upon Him while He is near. Let the wicked forsake his way, and the unrighteous man his thoughts; and let him return to the Lord, and He will have compassion on him; and to our God, for He will abundantly pardon."[8]

Footnotes to Chapter 11

1. Psalm 78:49
2. 2 Kings 19:32-37
3. 2 Samuel 24:15,16
4. Acts 12:21-24
5. Hebrews 10:31
6. Genesis 6:3
7. Hebrews 3:7
8. Isaiah 55:6,7

CHAPTER 12

Emergency Service

Perhaps the greatest and most extensive service rendered by the angels is that which is not recognized as such.

A missionary is burning up with fever in the heart of Africa. The only hope of saving his life is the application of ice packs. But the nearest ice is thousands of miles away. A desperate wife and fellow missionaries call upon a God who promised to be a very present help in time of trouble. Almost instantly dark storm clouds gather in the sky although that area is in the midst of the dry season. Thunders rumble and lightnings flash. And then it rains. Torrents of rain and the air is cooled. But God has more than rain to offer. Suddenly the missionaries are startled by a deafening drumming upon the tin roof of their home. *It is hail—ice—*tons of it! more than they could ever need! And it is gathered and applied, and the deadly fever is broken.

No, this is not fiction. It is fact. It happened. No one saw an angel, but who do you think gathered the clouds together and chilled the air currents to produce that hail? Is it not likely that the Holy Ones were sent to minister to those heirs of salvation in Africa?

In *A Prisoner and Yet*,[1] Corrie ten Boom tells of the angelic emergency service she received in a Nazi prison camp.

"Upon entering the camp we had to surrender not only our clothing but also our medicines. But we were allowed to keep a few toilet articles. My small bottle of Davitamon, a liquid vitamin compound, was then about half full. I set it down on the table, and the woman who was checking us in said: 'That is also a toilet article.'

"She put it back in my bag with her own hands, and I was very happy about it. Vitamin deficiency was one of the gravest hazards to the prisoners. From the very first day I gave everyone sleeping around me a couple drops of Davitamon daily. I gave it to as many as thirty persons at a time, but the little bottle continued to yield its drops. This went on for six or eight weeks, until the women no longer asked me, 'Do you still have some Davitamon?' but, 'Do you still have any oil from the cruse of the widow of Zarephath?'

"They were right in calling it that, for, as 'the jar of meal wasted not, neither did the cruse of oil fail, according to the word of Jehovah which He spake by Elijah,' so also were we experiencing a like miracle.

"Then one day my friend who worked in the hospital brought me a bagful of vitamins; I believe it was brewer's yeast. 'Give this to all the women around you,' said she. 'There is so much vitamin deficiency in camp. But do not tell anyone that I gave it to you.' So I gave each woman enough to last her for a week.

"That evening I said to my sister, Betsie, 'I am going to give you Davitamon too as long as it lasts.' But not a drop came out of the bottle. The miracle was no longer necessary.

"The bag of vitamins was also blessed. There always seemed to be enough, until one evening someone asked me, 'Do you still have some vitamins?' 'No,' said I, 'I am very sorry, but it is all gone.'

"I still had a tiny bit left, but wanted to keep it for Betsie. Now I confessed to her, 'That really showed that I was lacking in faith. I should have been more confident and have given her the last little bit.' Scarcely were the words out of my mouth when I saw my friend from the hospital approaching. And she actually had another bagful of vitamins with her. It was a great miracle. Vitamins were hard to get throughout the entire camp. Even if a doctor felt they were necessary for some patient he wanted to favor, he would still frequently be unable to procure them. It is really not out of place to speak of the 'miracle of the vitamins.' "

Yes, Corrie, it was a great miracle wrought through the power of God. And probably God sent an angel to maintain the level in that bottle of Davitamon and also to show your friend from the hospital how

111

and where to secure those bags of vitamins. In fact, it is possibly true that behind every great miracle there is a Holy One who has been sent to minister to a need.

God works through men. This is especially true in this age in the field of evangelism. God has committed to us—to men and women—the ministry of reconciliation. He is pleased by the foolishness of preaching to save them that believe. It is equally true that in other areas of service, God uses angels. Eternity may reveal that God has always worked through creatures He has made and designed for specific ministries. We may discover that in many historical instances where our Bible speaks of action on the part of the Lord God, He gave the command, but a Holy One was entrusted with the responsibility of fulfilling it.

As an example, the word of the Lord came to Elijah the Tishbite, " 'Go away from here and turn eastward, and hide yourself by the brook Cherith, which is east of Jordan. And it shall be that you shall drink of the brook, and I have commanded the ravens to provide for you there'. . . . And the ravens brought him bread and meat in the morning and bread and meat in the evening."[2]

Who directed those irresponsible ravens? Who kept the ravens from eating the meat and bread themselves? Who steered them to that one brook, Cherith, and to the exact spot where the prophet was waiting? Who made those greedy birds surrender the meat and the bread to the man of God? Who saw that the ravens maintained a regular schedule? The only answer to all these questions is, of course, *the Holy*

Ones. God can do anything, and He usually does everything through His servants.

While serving as missionaries in Africa, my wife and I found it necessary to drive our old Chevy truck some four hundred kilometers to the nearest store to pick up some essential supplies. We took our youngsters along. On our return trip, while still over two hundred miles from our mission station, and in the middle of nowhere, suddenly the motor began to race but the truck stopped dead in its tracks. An examination indicated that the differential had given out. The nearest help was over two hundred miles away, and *on foot!* Our water and food supplies were limited. Back at Kamayala, desperately sick patients were waiting for the medical supplies we had picked up at Kikwit.

There was no help for us on earth but we did have an open line of communication with heaven, and we used it. We gathered around the old Chevy, and placing our hands upon it we prayed that God would heal it and let His angels bring us safely home. There was a united "Amen." We all clambered aboard, started the motor, put her into low gear, let out the clutch, and the truck moved, picked up speed and without faltering for one moment took us all the way home!

As I pulled up in back of our house, the motor began to race and the truck stopped! The following day when I disassembled the rear end, I found the rear axle was broken into two pieces! And it was not an angled break! There was no possible way that the old Chevy could have gone two inches, but it went over two hundred miles! I don't understand divine automotive mechanics, but I do know that somehow God's Holy Ones held those broken ends together until we arrived safely at home. We called upon heaven's Emergency Service and it proved to be a very present help in time of trouble.

Many times things just seem to happen. Pieces begin to fit together—call it happenstance if you will. But when pieces of time and places and people all are made to fit into a perfect pattern it is more likely to be action on the part of the Holy Ones.

Brother Andrew, in *God's Smuggler*,[3] tells how in one day he received an inner assurance that told him, "Today you are going to get the visa for Yugoslavia." Then came the letter from the Yugoslavian government informing him that his application for a visa had been denied. Immediately he rushed to the Yugoslavian consulate and within twenty minutes he was given his visa! And before the day was over he was given a Volkswagen by a neighbor who knew it would be useful in smuggling Bibles behind the Iron Curtain.

Brother Andrew's story continues:

"I spent several days planning my itinerary, scouring Amsterdam for any kind of Christian printed matter in Yugoslav languages, and going over the car for places to conceal what I found. I spent a little time, too, wondering how God was going to supply the money for this trip.

"The end of March was my target date. Before then I drove down to see Karl de Graaf. I couldn't wait to see his face when he saw the car—the visible proof of what he'd known only by faith till then.

"But Mr. de Graaf showed no surprise whatever.

'Yes,' he said, 'I thought you'd have it by now. Because,' he went on, drawing an envelope from his pocket, 'God has told us that you will be needing an additional sum of money these next two months. And here it is.'

"He placed the envelope in my hand. I didn't even open it. By now I knew enough of this remarkable group to be sure that the envelope contained precisely the amount I would need for the trip."

When Brother Andrew arrived at the Yugoslav border he prayed, "Lord, in my luggage I have Scripture that I want to take to Your children across this border. When You were on earth, You made blind eyes see. Now, I pray, make seeing eyes blind. Do not let the guards see those things You do not want them to see."

"When I drove up to the barrier one of the two guards began to examine my camping gear. In the corners and folds of my sleeping bag and tent were boxes of tracts. 'Lord, make those seeing eyes blind.'

"The other guard was looking inside the VW. He asked me to take out a suitcase. I knew there were tracts scattered through my clothing.

" 'Of course, sir,' I said. I pulled the front seat forward and dragged the suitcase out. I placed it on the ground and opened the lid. The guard lifted the shirts that lay on top. Beneath them, and now in plain sight, was a pile of tracts in two different Yugoslavian languages, Croatian and Slovene. How was God going to handle this situation?

" 'It seems dry for this time of year,' I said to the other guard, and without looking at the fellow who was inspecting the suitcase, I fell into a conversation about the weather. Finally when I could stand the suspense no longer, I looked behind me. The first guard wasn't even glancing at the suitcase. He was listening to our conversation. When I turned around he caught himself and looked up.

" 'Well then, do you have anything else to declare?'

" 'Only small things,' I said. The tracts were small after all.

" 'We won't bother with them,' said the guard. He nodded to me that I could close the suitcase, and with a little salute handed me back my passport."

Brother Andrew tells of an even more dramatic action on the part of heaven's Emergency Service when he attempted to smuggle Bibles into Romania.

"When I pulled up to the checkpoint on the other side of the Danube, I said to myself, 'Well, I'm in luck. Only half a dozen cars. This will go swiftly.'

"When forty minutes had passed and the first car was still being inspected, I thought, 'Poor fellow, they must have something on him to take so long.'

"But when that car finally left and the next inspection took half an hour too, I began to worry. Literally, everything that family was carrying had to be taken out and spread on the ground. Every car in the line was put through the same routine. The fourth inspection lasted for well over an hour. The guards took the driver inside and kept him there while they removed hub caps, took his engine apart, removed seats.

" 'Dear Lord,' I said, as at last there was just one car ahead of me, 'what am I going to do? Any serious inspection will show up those Romanian Bibles right away.'

" 'Lord,' I went on, 'I know that no amount of

116

cleverness on my part can get me through this border search. Dare I ask for a miracle? Let me take some of the Bibles out and leave them in the open where they can be seen. Then, Lord, I cannot possibly be depending on my own stratagems, can I? I will be depending utterly upon You.' "

"While the last car was going through its chilling inspection, I managed to take several Bibles from their hiding places and pile them on the seat beside me.

"It was my turn. I put the little VW in low gear, inched up to the officer standing at the left side of the road, handed him my papers, and started to get out. But his knee was against the door, holding it closed. He looked at my photograph in the passport, scribbled something down, shoved the papers back under my nose, and abruptly waved me on.

"Surely thirty seconds had not passed. I started the engine and inched forward, my foot above the brake. Nothing happened. I looked out the rear mirror. The guard was waving the next car to a stop, indicating to the driver that he had to get out. I had made it through that incredible checkpoint in the space of thirty seconds!"[4]

In these experiences of Brother Andrew we have a Communist government refusing and then granting a visa the same day; a car is given; expense money is provided; and a border guard is blinded to Bible literature in plain view! Time, places and people are fit together and a beautiful design of God's providence is completed. Heaven's Emergency Service has brought another assignment to a successful conclusion.

117

Footnotes to Chapter 12

1. Corrie ten Boom, *A Prisoner and Yet* (Fort Washington, Pa.: Christian Literature Crusade, 1954).
2. 1 Kings 17:1-6
3. Brother Andrew, *God's Smuggler* (Old Tappan, N.J.: Fleming H. Revell Co., 1968).
4. Brother Andrew, *God's Smuggler.*

The Hallelujah Chorus

In the preceding chapters we have examined the ministries of the Holy Ones in the infallible record of God's Word. We have seen their power displayed in judgment and divine vengeance upon God's enemies, and in the deliverance and protection of the heirs of salvation.

As our final thought regarding the Holy Ones, we will permit the Psalmist and the apostle John to direct our attention to another function of the angels; one in which they excel and in which the human children of God are very deficient—the art of praise.

Here, there are few stories to relate, because this activity of the Holy Ones is related only to God. However, as we observe their fidelity and joy in this function, it can and should challenge us to join with them in this highest of all forms of worship.

It is indeed fitting that it should have been the

Psalmist who called our attention to this angelic activity. More than any other mortal, David, the sweet singer of Israel, exercised and developed the art of praise approaching nearest to possible perfection on the human plane.

As David remembered the goodness of God and contemplated on the wonder of His grace and the majesty of His power, and in the ecstasy of this wonder, he cried out,

"Praise the Lord!
Praise the Lord from the heavens;
Praise Him in the heights!
Praise Him, all His angels;
Praise Him, all His hosts!
Praise Him, sun and moon;
Praise Him, all stars of light!
Praise Him, highest heavens,
And the waters that are above the heavens!
Let them praise the name of the Lord,
For He commanded and they were created."[1]

Upon another occasion, as the Psalmist meditated upon the Lord's mercies, there was born in his grateful heart a most beautiful song. Recalling his own blemished past and remembering how he had to throw himself upon the mercy of God, he seemed to feel he could not adequately express his gratitude. He needed help—the help of the Holy Ones—only they, in their angels' tongues, could say that which never could be said in the tongues of men. So, appealing to them, David cried, "Bless the Lord, you His angels, mighty in strength, who perform His word, obeying the voice of His word! Bless the Lord, all you His hosts, you who serve Him, doing His will."[2]

And there can be no doubt that they did, and are doing just that not only in heaven, but also are bringing some of that spirit of praise into human situations on earth. There is a blessed promise in Isaiah, "Giving . . . a garland instead of ashes, the oil of gladness instead of mourning, the mantle of praise instead of a spirit of fainting."[3] Let me tell you of a documented instance when a Holy One brought a fulfillment of this promise to a family standing in desperate need of the spirit of praise.

For many years Mr. and Mrs. Charles Pereau, of North Hollywood, California, had been very close friends of a saint of God, Rev. Reid Lunsford, who spent the last years of his life in Phoenix, Arizona. He had been a Southern Baptist minister for many years and also founded the Highways and Hedges Mission in Phoenix.

Upon receiving word that Rev. Lunsford's condition had taken a turn for the worse, the Pereaus went to see him. A few days after they arrived he had a serious attack and it became evident that his earthly course had been run. It was a time of great sorrow for the family and friends gathered about the bed. Mrs. Pereau describes the events:

"Tears flowed freely and some of us were sobbing in our grief. My husband began to sing, 'I Come to the Garden Alone.' "

"At that moment I happened to look across the room and at the end of the room there was standing a creature of light. He was very tall—it seemed that he was too tall to stand in that room. He was not transparent but rather three dimensional. I was first impressed by the glorious whiteness of his person—the purest and whitest white one could imagine. Yet through the whiteness there shone a beautiful iridescence displaying every color of the rainbow.

"I wanted to call the attention of the others to this glorious person but I was speechless. At that moment Rev. Lunsford breathed his last breath and a look of beautiful peace came upon his face—almost a radiance. I looked up but the creature of light had disappeared!

"Later that evening, the daughter of Rev. Lunsford who had been standing beside me, and was facing in the same direction when I saw that shining person, came to me and said, 'Did you see that magnificent light that appeared at the other end of the room right before Daddy died?'

"I asked, 'Was it a light that you saw, June?'

" 'Well, it had form—it was the most beautiful light I have ever seen, but it did have form—something like you would think an angel would appear.'

"Then I told her what I had seen. The strangest phenomenon was not the appearance of that glorious person of light but the instantaneous removal of all sorrow and grief from that room of death at the moment of his appearance. All weeping and sobbing ceased and everyone began to praise the Lord and rejoice. A peace that was almost tangible filled every heart. It was as though the great hand of God had reached down and wiped away every tear.

"We sat down and began to sing hymns of victory and praise. That strange atmosphere of peace and praise continued all through the following days and into the memorial service. There seemed to be an ineffable glory and lovely fragrance filling every room in that home and it lingered on for weeks after the friends had left.

"Was that glorious creature an angel sent to escort our beloved friend into the presence of his Lord? Or, was it a ministering spirit sent to impart peace— 'giving them a garland instead of ashes, the oil of gladness instead of mourning, the mantle of praise instead of a spirit of fainting'?"

Yes, in heaven and on earth the Holy Ones are engaged in the ministry of praise. In fact, when the apostle John was transported into the presence of God, he witnessed the angelic hosts engaged in this glorious function. And what a sight and what a sound that must have been! Describing his experience, John wrote:

"And I looked, and I heard the voice of many angels around the throne and the living creatures and the elders; and the number of them was myriads of myriads, and thousands of thousands; saying with a loud voice,

" 'Worthy is the Lamb that was slain to receive power and riches and wisdom and might and honor and glory and blessing.' "[4]

But that was only the first stanza of the angels' "Hallelujah Chorus." All the angels then gathered "around the throne and around the elders and the four living creatures; and they fell on their faces before the throne and worshiped God, saying,

" 'Amen, blessing and glory and wisdom and thanksgiving and honor and power and might, be to our God forever and ever. Amen.' "[5]

Yes, heaven is a place of praise!—where there is no complaining, no gossip, no angry words, no fears nor tensions—where there is only praise—forever and ever!

Regarding these four living creatures of heaven, John said they were a chorus or quartet of chanters. "Day and night they do not cease to say, 'Holy, holy, holy, is the Lord God, the Almighty, who was and who is and who is to come.' And . . . the living creatures give glory and honor and thanks to Him who sits on the throne, to Him who lives forever and ever."[6]

How different earth is from heaven! On earth we hear people damn God and we see them scorn His proffered grace. Even in Christian circles seldom can one find a note of praise. Our prayers consist largely of requests for personal grants. Our attitudes reflect discontent. We radiate unhappiness and fears.

I have an idea that as the Holy Ones observe us, they turn sadly to each other and say, "Oh, that men would praise the Lord for his goodness, and for his wonderful works to the children of man!"[7]

There is a third stanza to the angels' "Hallelujah Chorus." The Holy Ones came down on earth to sing it, and the world has never been the same since! It happened almost two thousand years ago. The stage for the sacred concert was the shepherds' fields near Bethlehem. And by this time, we are quite familiar with that third stanza but we seldom sing it. Let us refreshen ourselves with the words of Luke:

"And suddenly there appeared with the angel a multitude of the heavenly host praising God, and saying, 'Glory to God in the highest, and on earth peace among men with whom He is pleased.' "[8]

Why wait until Christmas to sing it? Join with the

Holy Ones and sing it now—today and tomorrow—let it fill your mind and motivate your life, every day of your life! Think it. Pray it. Tell it wherever you go, "Glory to God in the highest."

Then stand alongside of David, and sing with him the refrain,

"I will bless the Lord at all times, His praise shall continually be in my mouth. My soul shall make its boast in the Lord; the humble shall hear it and rejoice. O magnify the Lord with me, and let us exalt His name together.

"I sought the Lord, and He answered me, and delivered me from all my fears. They looked to Him and were radiant, and their faces shall never be ashamed. This poor man cried and the Lord heard him; and saved him out of all his troubles. The angel of the Lord encamps around those who fear Him, and rescues them."[9]

Footnotes to Chapter 13

1. Psalm 148:1-5
2. Psalm 103:20,21
3. Isaiah 61:3
4. Revelation 5:11,12
5. Revelation 7:11,12
6. Revelation 4:8,9
7. Psalm 107:8, *King James Version*
8. Luke 2:13,14
9. Psalm 34:1-7

Bibliography

Andrew, Brother. *God's Smuggler.* Old Tappan, New Jersey: Fleming H. Revell Co., 1968.

Beale, William James. *Divine Causation;* a critical study concerning "intermediaries." London: Macmillan & Co., limited, 1937, 335 p.

Blunt, John Henry. *Dictionary of Doctrinal and Historical Theology.* Second Edition. London: Rivingtons, 1872, 825 p.

Bruce, Alexander Balmain. *The Providential Order of the World.* New York: C. Scribner's Sons, 1897, 346 p.

Chambers, Oswald. *Workmen of God;* the cure of souls. New York: Grosset and Dunlap, 1938, 115 p.

D'Arcy, Charles Frederick. *Providence and the World Order.* London: Hodder and Stoughton, limited, 1932, 254 p.

DuBose, Horace M. *The Consciousness of Jesus.* New York, Cincinnati: The Methodist Book Concern; Nashville, Dallas: Smith and Lamar, 1917.

Fowler, Alfred. *Our Angel Friends in Ministry and Song.* Philadelphia, no publisher listed, 1903.

Gaebelein, Arno Clemens. *The Angels of God.* New York: Publication Office "Our Hope", 1924, 116 p.

Gaebelein, Arno Clemens. *Gabriel and Michael.* New York: Our Hope Publications (A. C. Gaebelein, Inc.), 1945, 135 p.

Heidt, Rev. William George. *Angelology of the Old Testament.* Catholic University of America Press, 1949, 119 p.

Lange, Johann Peter. *The Life of the Lord Jesus Christ.* Edinburgh, T. & T. Clark, 1864, 6 volumes.

Langton, Edward. *The Angel Teaching of the New Testament.* London: James Clarke, no date, 224 p.

Langton, Edward. *Essentials of Demonology* (a study of Jewish and Christian doctrine, its origin and development). London: Epworth Press, 1949, 234 p. (Continuation of the author's *Good and Evil Spirits).*

Langton, Edward. *Good and Evil Spirits.* London: Society for Promoting Christian Knowledge; New York: Macmillan Co., 1942, 324 p.

Langton, Edward. *The Ministries of the Angelic Powers According to the Old Testament and Later Jewish Literature.* London: J. Clarke and Co., limited, 1936, 189 p.

Lewis, C. S. *The Screwtape Letters.* New York: Macmillan Co., 1969.

Lockyer, Herbert. *The Mystery and Ministry of Angels.* Grand Rapids: Eerdmans Publishing Co., 1958, 96 p.

McClintock Strong. *Cyclopedia of Biblical Theological and Ecclesiastical Literature.* Grand Rapids: Baker Book House, 1891.

ten Boom, Corrie. *A Prisoner and Yet.* Fort Washington, Pa.: Christian Literature Crusade, 1954.

ten Boom, Corrie. *Marching Orders for the End Battle.* Fort Washington, Pa.: Christian Literature Crusade, 1969.

Whately, Richard. *A View of the Scripture Revelations Respecting Good and Evil Angels.* Second Edition. Philadelphia: Lindsay and Blakiston, 1856, 174 p.

Whyte, Alexander. *The Nature of Angels.* London: Hodder and Stoughton, limited, 1930, 221 p.